RESTORING THE CENTER

ESSAYS EVANGELICAL & ECUMENICAL

Gabriel Fackre

InterVarsity Press
Downers Grove, Illinois

InterVarsity Press
P.O. Box 1400, Downers Grove, IL 60515
World Wide Web: www.ivpress.com
E-mail: mail@ivpress.com

InterVarsity Press® *is the book-publishing division of InterVarsity Christian Fellowship/USA*®, *a student movement active on campus at hundreds of universities, colleges and schools of nursing in the United States of America, and a member movement of the International Fellowship of Evangelical Students. For information about local and regional activities, write Public Relations Dept., InterVarsity Christian Fellowship/USA, 6400 Schroeder Rd., P.O. Box 7895, Madison, WI 53707-7895.*

Scripture quotations, unless otherwise noted, are from the New Revised Standard Version of the Bible, *copyright 1989 by the Division of Christian Education of the National Council of the Churches of Christ in the USA. Used by permission. All rights reserved.*

Cover photograph: Thia Konig

ISBN 0-8308-1508-2

Printed in the United States of America ♻

Library of Congress Cataloging-in-Publication Data

Fackre, Gabriel J.
    Restoring the center : essays evangelical and ecumenical / Gabriel
Fackre.
        p.   cm.
    Includes bibliographical references.
    ISBN 0-8308-1508-2 (pbk. : alk. paper)
    1. Ecumenical movement.   2. Evangelicalism.   I. Title.
BX9.F27   1998
277.3'0829—dc21   98-24543
                                                                                                              CIP

18	17	16	15	14	13	12	11	10	9	8	7	6	5	4	3	2	1
13	12	11	10	09	08	07	06	05	04	03	02	01	00	99	98		

Preface   7

Part I

Retrospective: Patterns of Twentieth-Century Theology

1 Theology Ephemeral & Durable   *11*

Part II

Signs of Recentering

2 The Church of the Center   *27*

3 Centralities in the Parish   *46*

4 Centralities in the Seminaries   *57*

5 I Believe in the Resurrection of the Body   *66*

6 Angels Heard & Demons Seen   *78*

Part III

Ecumenical & Evangelical Explorations

7 In Quest of the Comprehensive: The Systematics Revival   *95*

8 An Altar Call for Evangelicals   *112*

9 Whither Evangelicalism?   *119*

10 The New Ecumenism: Mutual Affirmation & Admonition   *123*

Part IV

The Search for the Center in Ethics & Institutions

11 IBM & the Incognito Christ   *135*

12 Preaching on Abortion   *144*

13 The Continuing Relevance of Reinhold Niebuhr   *149*

14 Seminary Cultures—Evangelical & Mainline   *161*

Notes   *171*

95053

Preface

The new century . . . the new millennium . . . the new age . . . The rush is on to say what is to come. Futurists, millenarians religious and secular, hustlers of products pious and political have found a *fin de siècle* market for their nostrums. I began my own odyssey in futurology some years ago as a member of the World Future Society and one of the organizers of a Conference on "Religion and the Future."[1] Living over time with future-talk, however, brings its lessons, and with them a sobering of hope.

While future-orientation is inextricable from Christian faith, the Not Yet is grounded in an Already. What is to come is rooted in what has been and is: ultimately the person and work of Jesus Christ; penultimately, the work of the Holy Spirit in historical currents past and present. The prospective needs a retrospective. Without it new century/millennium/age projections are only our favorite fancies. Mea culpa for muting the givens of the past in my own earlier enthusiasms. This book is an argument for remembering. Its essays reflect one theologian's effort to bring vision in closer touch with reality/Reality.

Evangelical readers will find in this retrospective mainline-church paths pursued that could have been forecast as dead ends. At the same time, a new breed of evangelical eager to be in touch with culture may have something to learn from both the mistakes made and the new directions charted by the "ecumenicals" considered here. Indeed, the writer believes that the end of the century is a special moment of opportunity for an evangelical-ecumenical alliance.[2]

Restoring the Center, with its hopes for tomorrow, is first and foremost an orientation to the ultimate *Already,* Jesus Christ. Each issue taken up is read christologically—who is Jesus Christ for us today?—in the cacophony of angel talk, in strategies for social change, in movements of church renewal, in the rise of evangelicalism, in the surge of systematic theology, in seminary culture wars, in new frontiers in ecumenism. So many voices telling us where we must go! May they not drown out "the one Word" we have "to hear and obey . . . Jesus Christ as attested by Holy Scripture." So Barmen's counsel and warning to us in the fiercest church struggle of the century. At that 1934 Synod, Confessing Christians in Germany stood against Hitler's blood-and-soil philosophy. Surrounded by our own more subtle ideologies, we also need to be reclaimed by *Christ the Center,* as Dietrich Bonhoeffer who died in that struggle expressed it.

This end-of-century quest for the Center takes up learnings from a more recent past as well as from the Ancient of Days. Preparing for a new agenda means reading the minutes of the last meeting. This book is a retrospective in that sense as well, a look at some lessons of twentieth-century theology that are easily forgotten by those mesmerized by the twenty-first. Hence the chapter on fifty years of theology that traces twentieth-century reductionist temptations. And some similar advice for ebullient evangelicals treading the same minefields traversed earlier by ecumenicals. And some reminders of reality for us all from one of the century's giants, Reinhold Niebuhr.

Recentering means focus on the "centralities" as well as the Center. Jesus Christ is the central chapter of a Story that runs from creation to consummation. Each chapter is a *locus,* a "place" in history, where God did, does and will deal with us. Christian rumination about these places becomes a *theological* locus in both the teaching ministry of a congregation and in the systematics classroom in seminary. Part of the trajectory of the recent past into the twenty-first century is the retrieval of this narrative of faith. Here the recovery of the centralities is noted in chapters on Christian education and the discipline of systematic theology.

Recentering at end-of-century has to do with the emergence of an *ecclesial* center. A "centrist" movement is struggling to be born in the mainline churches, marked by determined confession of the one Word, Jesus Christ, and the recovery of the Great Narrative. As such, is it the institutional expression of lessons learned by the close of this de-centered century and a portent of things to come? May God grant that it be so.

Part I
Retrospective:
Patterns of
Twentieth-Century
Theology

---

*A survey of some fifty years of personal involvement in
theological currents of the twentieth century allows lessons to be
drawn for the twenty-first-century church. The occasion for the
retrospective was an alumni/ae gathering of the writer's former
Andover Newton students.*

1

Theology Ephemeral & Durable[†]

FIFTY YEARS OF THEOLOGY, MISSION, MINISTRY . . . WHAT DO WE MAKE OF IT at end-of-century? Specifically: What happened to theology, mission and ministry in the "mainline" churches and their seminary counterparts?

An image from a school of French cultural historians helps orient us.[1] Fernand Braudel, Pierre Chaunu and François Furet read history as if it were three associated wheels of varying sizes spinning at different rates. A larger wheel turns very, very slowly—a "structural" history in which change is infinitesimal. A middle-size wheel turns faster, representing trends that alter but persist over long periods— "conjunctural" history. And a smaller wheel goes very, very fast through rapidly changing times—"ephemeral" history.

The structural, conjunctural and ephemeral were all present in the past half-century of "mainstream" theology. The outer wheel of perduring Christian theology and perennial Christian conviction left its

†This essay was a presentation to alumni/ae of Andover Newton Theological School, June 3, 1996.

mark among us. The middle wheel of theology shaped by the two-hundred-year period of the Enlightenment was deeply formative. But it was the inner wheel, with elements from the other two, that best characterized the age.

The predominance of the ephemeral in the last half-century of theology reflects the culture's own swift movements—"rapidation" as sociologists describe it. Such alacrity lends credence to a dividing of the half-century into decades—the fifties, sixties, seventies . . . (as in David Halberstam's *The Fifties*[2]). Of course these divisions for both American culture and theology are overly simple; turning points do not come on Day One of a new decade. But a ten-year taxonomy does point to discernible tendencies.

As a footnote to this changing scene, I offer evidence here from my own personal struggle to *relate* but not *capitulate* to the ever-new contexts—battles, as can be seen, that were both lost and won.

The 1950s

Paul Tillich—a figure who influenced the worlds of art, philosophy and psychology as well as theology—was a name on many lips in this decade. Tillich held that the Christian message must be correlated with an era's cultural question.[3] In the post–World War II period the existentialist Tillich formulated the issue variously as anxiety, meaninglessness, dread, dehumanization, despair and death. He tailored his theology accordingly, speaking the therapeutic word of healing to our estrangement. Christ became the *New Being* who answered our agonies of *nonbeing*. His diagnosis struck a chord in many people haunted by the prospects of World War III, shaped by the worlds of "organization man" and "the lonely crowd" (popular books of the period), a macerated, mobile mass society with its impersonal institutions—big industry, big unions, big government, big media . . .

The Tillichian existential theology was partnered in many places with a formative missiology. What was the church for? Why, *koinonia*, of course. In a footloose depersonalized world we can get back our name and face through the *fellowship* of the congregation. Indeed, the "fellowship hall" was often the first unit of the many new churches built in the exploding suburbs of the 1950s. In a larger sense, as Will Herberg said in his widely read book, *Protestant,*

Catholic, Jew,[4] Americans found personal meaningfulness and identity in these broad religious communities. As if to prove the conjunction of inner-peace-seeking and religious tradition, Roman Catholic Fulton Sheen wrote *Peace of Soul,* Rabbi Joshua Liebman, *Peace of Mind,* and Billy Graham, *Peace with God.* Thus a popular theology and piety diagnosed the cultural problem in ways parallel to Tillich, albeit prescribing quite differently.

A personal note: The Fackres—Gabriel, Dorothy and a newborn daughter—left the University of Chicago Divinity School in 1951 for an industrial parish in Pittsburgh fired up by the previous decade's social action agenda. In 1948 we had toured Great Britain on bicycles studying "the Church and the Working-classes," mentored by social ethicist James Luther Adams. We were determined to be in solidarity with blue-collar America, regularly neglected by mainstream Christianity. We were scornful of the popular bourgeois peace-of-mind religion, and rejected, as well, Tillich's theology and therapeutics.

We spent ten exciting and demanding years in that mill-town parish. But as the decade wore on, "mission" came to be less and less the struggle for worker rights and more and more a proletarian version of the age's "quest for community." What the church could do for the alienated worker was to be a place where John and Jane Doe got back their names and faces. No longer button numbers at the mill gate, they could experience a singling-out love—God's and their fellow members'—in the beloved community. *Koinonia* became our watchword. Our most passionate commitment in the final years was not marching on U.S. Steel to fight layoffs at the Homestead works (although we did play a small role with other mill-town pastors in the 1959 steel strike), but rather creating a seventy-five-acre parish retreat center out in the country—the "Milliron Community," modeled on Scotland's pioneering Iona Community—for workers and their families. For Dot and myself, the Mercersburg theology shaped an important church doctrine and gave support to this concept—the church as "the realm of redemption." Together we wrote our first book, *Under the Steeple,*[5] echoing just these themes. While never Tillichians, our own ministry was evidence of the postwar problematic of "estrangement." And the answer to this cultural question, while not philosophically the Tillich-based solution of *New Being,* was the *new being-together* of Christian community.

The 1960s

In the 1960s mainstream theology in the United States took a significant turn away from the anxieties, interiorities and together-nesses of the 1950s. Roger Shinn, Union Seminary colleague of Paul Tillich, commented in the fall of 1963 on a new student mood: "For many of our students the time had come to break the prolonged mood of introspection . . . the fashionable reveling in anxiety. . . . [They] learned instead to march and sing! This has been the time when the American ear . . . heard the clear strains of 'We shall overcome someday!'"[6] The change was symbolized by the March on Washington with its memorable speech by Martin Luther King Jr.—not "I have a despair," but "I have a dream!"

Political dream, social hope, the vision and promise of the Not Yet became key words in the lexicon of both church and culture. Not *present*-oriented inner anxieties, but a future-oriented, history-directed hope for a renewed society, and a *world*-drenched mission for the church. American theology, continuing to be influenced by European thinkers (this time Jürgen Moltmann and Wolfhart Pannenberg[7]), had its own counterpart theologies of hope and the future. But it was a North American *activist* version of futuring that claimed the spotlight. Harvey Cox's bestselling book *The Secular City*[8] was the megaphone. What was out there and ahead in human history counted the most. Not Tillich's "ultimate concern," but Martin Luther King's penultimate hope. Not the church-centered koinonia of the 1950s, but the world-oriented diakonia of the 1960s. Not the "nonbeing" of personal death but the "being, having and belonging" (war, poverty, race), the social death and new hope for peace and justice.

And, it was said with great passion, we needed new forms of mission commensurate with that turn. Not the "hatching, matching and dispatching"—baptism, marriage, burial—of ordinary congregations, presumed now to be obsolete . . . not the churchy "come" word of the 1950s: "Come unto me all you who are heavy laden, and I will give you rest," but the liberating, worldly "go" word of the 1960s: "Go into all the world!" "God so loved the world!" "You are the light of the world!"

Was it any accident that Dietrich Bonhoeffer came to the fore in much North American theology of that era, especially in his *Letters and Papers from Prison*?[9] Executed by the Nazis for his part in the underground confessing church movement, writing about a new kind of Christianity—a church *for others* that moved out onto secular terrain to "participate in the sufferings of God in the *world*"—a Christianity that refused to exploit our anxieties, rejoicing instead in the world's "coming of age," a world now expected to solve its own problems without benefit of the "god-of-the-gaps." For all that, Bonhoeffer was a devout believer—something forgotten by many of his popularizers—but he taught that the place for the celebration of orthodox faith was in the *disciplina arcani,* a "hidden discipline" in a catacombs church, while up on the surface in the secular world a silent "Christian presence" in simple acts of mercy and justice was the meaning of mission.

As might have been predicted, sensational versions of this accent on secularity soon appeared: the "death of God theology" with its three media-courted figures, Paul van Buren, Thomas Altizer and William Hamilton; a "death of code" morality associated with the "situation ethics" of Joseph Fletcher; and a "death of church" ecclesiology detailed by church sociologists like Gibson Winter, who sought new forms of secular mission. The theological writings of Anglican bishop J. A. T. Robinson, as in his widely read book *Honest to God,*[10] brought all three accents together.

Modest versions of the refrains of the 1960s could be seen in Roman Catholicism, especially in the Second Vatican Council's responding to John XXIII's call to "open a window" to the world and let its fresh breezes ventilate the stuffy church. Hints of more drastic things to come could be found in the early works of two then-Roman Catholic women theologians, Mary Daly and Rosemary Radford Ruether, both of whom helped lay the foundations for a new theological feminism.

Of course, as in the 1950s, so in the 1960s, there were significant circles of theology and church life largely unaffected by or resistant to these developments: in Eastern Orthodoxy, conservative evangelical, Calvinist and Lutheran circles, for example. There were signs, too, of restiveness with the secular assumptions and countermovement in the churches, as in the polarization in the late 1960s between "hippie" and "hardhat" constituencies and theologies. But the focal point of "theology, mission and ministry" for many in mainline theology and church life in both North America and Europe was epitomized by the influential World Council of Churches' study book with its Bonhoefferesque title *The Church for Others*,[11] and its call for the church to seek the "humanization" of the world.

A personal note: In 1961, the Fackres (husband, wife and now four children) moved from mill-town to middle America, from preaching in Pittsburgh to teaching at Lancaster Theological Seminary. In 1963, when Shinn and his students began "to march and sing," so did the Fackres—in that King-led 1963 March on Washington and at countless demonstrations in Lancaster, in Canton, Mississippi, and elsewhere. Dot helped to desegregate the Lancaster public schools with her cadre of teachers in eight freedom schools housed in city congregations. I helped to organize a center-city coffee house, Encounter. Both of us were on the organizing committee of a citizen's newspaper formed to challenge the town's media monopoly. The books written in the 1960s echoed all these themes: *Secular Impact*,[12] a United Churches of Christ (UCC) study book titled *The Pastor and the World*,[13] a Bonhoeffer-inspired work (though critical of the three death-of-God, -code, -church theologies), *Humiliation and Celebration*,[14] and a volume on the theology of hope, *The Rainbow Sign*.[15] I also participated in the World Council of Churches' North American study group with Harvey Cox, Gibson Winter, Letty Russell, Colin Williams, Robert Spike, Andrew Young and other self-described "young Turks" that produced materials for a book called *The Church for Others*.

But all this with a difference. It had to do with the catholicity of the Mercersburg theology and an unswerving commitment to "the basics": don't throw the baby out with the bathwater; keep the whole of faith in sight while stressing the part. New forms yes, but don't forget the durable old ones, especially the congregation. Do worldly celebrative banners and buttons, but hang them on the walls of St. John's-by-the-Gas-Station. I believe we were beginning to learn something in the feverish 1960s: not only how to answer the culture's questions, but also how to question the culture's answers.

The 1970s

The writings of Harvey Cox are a barometer of North American theological weather. He scouted out the secular 1960s, but "the times they were 'a changin'." In 1969, Cox wrote *Feast of Fools*,[16] followed in 1973 by *Seduction of the Spirit*[17] and in 1977 *Turning East*.[18] They all reflected the decade's neomystical and Aquarian trends in both culture and church, along with its developing theologies of play, personal testimony (an early version of "story" theology) and pluralism. Meanwhile on the larger North American landscape, the neo-evangelical movement was gaining ground, initially with the appearance of the ex-hippie "Jesus freaks." In all these cases "religion" was once again having its day, or more exactly "religious experience." So Andrew Greeley announced in his book *Unsecular Man*.[19] Tracking the changes in words made familiar in World Council of Churches' studies, *leitourgia*—prayer, worship, spirituality—began to replace the previous decades' *koinonia* and *diakonia*.

The shape this took in academic theology was increasingly influenced by the emerging "religious studies" programs in colleges and universities. In them the particularities of Christian theology began to be nudged aside by "world religions" and the sociological study of the effects of "religion." In Christian theology there was a comparable accommodating response to these trends in the pluralist theologies of John Hick and Wilfred Cantwell Smith.

The more central stream of Christian theology in the 1970s attempted to honor a universal religious sensibility, the place of spirituality and the role of world religions, but to assert some kind of Christian particularity as in Karl Rahner and his "anonymous Christianity." Hans Küng and David Tracy, two other increasingly prominent Roman Catholic theologians, while critical of Rahner, worked with a similar commitment to a foundational religious experience. Further to the right in the spectrum of Christian theology, religious affect in general became the very specific charismatic and Pentecostal Christian experience, with their correlative movements. Both universal religious experience and its more specific Christian charismatic expression gave new impetus to the doctrine of the Holy Spirit and thus a wave of books on the neglected Third Person of the Trinity.

This momentum toward "the recovery of the sacred" (the name of a Notre Dame conference in the 1970s organized by Albert Outler) carried many toward an apolitical theology. Not so, Harvey Cox. Nor, in more substantial works such as *Jesus* and *Christ*, did Roman Catholic theologian Edward Schillebeeckx.[20] Both sought to combine the experiential with a call of believers to the liberating reign of God.

"Liberation!" For all the stress on the sacred that marked the times, another theological movement was gathering force in this decade, reflecting the growing diversity in the patterns of North American theology. With impulses from Latin America, especially in the writings of Gustavo Gutiérrez, a 1970s "liberation theology" elbowed aside the reformist 1960s "humanization theology," at least within the continuing politically antiestablishment segments of North American theology. It could be seen also in the move from Martin King to James Cone with the latter's *Black Theology and Black Power,*[21] and *A Black Theology of Liberation.*[22] North American Hispanic theology had its early representative in Orlando Costas, whose groundbreaking book *The Church and Its Mission*[23] brought liberation and evangelical witness together. And feminist theology was coming into its own in this period. While Mary Daly now moved *Beyond God the Father*[24] and into *Gyn/Ecology: The Metaethics of Radical Feminism,*[25] Letty Mandeville Russell stayed within the church with her *Human Liberation in a Feminist Perspective*[26] and set the agenda for a church debate on inclusive language with *The Liberating Word.*[27] Meanwhile, feminist studies of Scripture were pioneered by Phyllis Trible's *God and the Rhetoric of Sexuality*[28] and took new directions in Elisabeth Schüssler Fiorenza's *In Memory of Her.*[29]

In other quarters there was increasing uneasiness with the trends of the times, as in the growing criticism of liberation and feminist theologies in the writings of Cardinal Ratzinger. Indeed, former 1960s Roman Catholic radical Michael Novak became think-tank neoconservative Michael Novak. Antiwar activist Richard John Neuhaus joined the same ranks, and in the 1990s he joined the Church of Rome.

A personal note: The Fackres arrived January 1, 1971, at Andover Newton Theological School. We had been on a six-month interim stint at the University of Hawaii, having our first taste of both the neomysticisms and neopietisms of the changing times. In our last week in Honolulu we witnessed a confrontation on the streets of Waikiki between the devotees of Hari Krishna chanting "Krishna, Krishna, hari, hari" and a band of Jesus freaks singing at the top of their lungs "Onward Christian Soldiers." The era of religious energies, spirituality and evangelism had begun in earnest. These turns posed the issue for many of us in the mainline: had we in the 1960s been so fixed upon the *deed* of mercy and justice that we neglected the *word* of faith? Had our reductionism invited this reaction? Had mission been reduced to social action, ignoring evangelism? Had we neglected to "tell our Story"?

Some of us were convinced we had bread for the spiritual hunger of the day. But it could not be passed out the way the big evangelistic movement "Key 73" was doing it—just stressing the religious and personal side of mission. We were wary too of the popular apolitical mysticisms and pietisms. Perhaps we were learning a little more again about how "to relate but not capitulate" to the world's agenda. Thus was born in some mission circles what was called "Word in deed" evangelism: speaking the word of faith in the context of the deed of justice and mercy. We must break our silence and tell our Story, but do so in "Storyland." In the midst of the immediate social struggles. I wrote some little books on that theme, *Do and Tell*[30] and *Word in Deed.*[31] Dot made banners and designed buttons with that partnership in mind. At the same time, both of us became more and more convinced that in the 1950s and 1960s, indeed in raising our own children, we had stressed the church-for-the-world but had muted the word of faith. So in 1972, on the occasion of daughter Skye's confirmation, we together wrote for *Youth* magazine "A Catechism for Today's Storytellers."[32] The metaphor "story" that I began to use in an adult confirmation book written for the UCC in 1968, *Conversation in Faith,*[33] came to play an increasingly central role in my teaching and finally in the publication in 1978 of the first edition of a mini-systematics, *The Christian Story.*[34] Students need straight theology! Doctrine! Strange words for a secular or a mystical era. But just wait.

The 1980s

A slender volume appeared in 1984 to which theologians of the 1980s returned ever and again: *The Nature of Doctrine.*[35] In it Yale Divinity

School's George Lindbeck sounded notes similar to an earlier work by his colleague Hans Frei, *The Eclipse of the Biblical Narrative.*[36] Lindbeck and Frei argued that it was time to reclaim our own Christian language and its grammatical rules—classical Christian doctrine. Yes, use the wisdom of the culture but do it selectively, always making sure that the world of the Bible "absorbs" the extrabiblical world. Let the *church,* not the world, write the agenda—an absolute reversal of the conventional missiological wisdom of the 1960s. The work of Frei and Lindbeck and their students—Ronald Thiemann, Stanley Hauerwas, William Placher, George Hunsinger, Kathryn Tanner, Garrett Green et al.—came to be known as "the Yale theology," or more broadly as "postliberal" theology, with its rejection of Enlightenment premises and the recovery of the "biblical narrative." With this plea "not to be conformed to this world," Karl Barth was clearly lurking in the wings. Barth influenced postliberal (and some "postmodern") theologians but also was rediscovered by others increasingly wary of the cultural captivity of the church.

The stress on Christian particularity and the retrieval of Christian language and tradition were manifest in a number of other theological developments of the 1980s. In Roman Catholicism a self-defined "centrist" constituency became more vocal, one committed to the second Vatican Council's advances but worried about the loss in post-Vatican II theology of the dogmatic tradition. Thus Avery Dulles, who had stressed the many models of church, began to advocate more and more a return to tradition. And Raymond Brown, on the cutting edge of critical scholarship, expressed increasing concern about directions in his own church and urged loyalty to the magisterium. An evangelical catholic movement came to higher profile in the Reformation churches, also stressing the recovery of dogmatic tradition, sacraments and a teaching office, as in the work of Carl Braaten and Robert Jenson.

The attempt to ground "relevance" in foundational Christian "identity" was evident in the day-to-day life of congregations, as in the renewed emphasis on preaching and teaching and the increased use of the lectionary. Thus *kerygma*—the telling of the Story that had been muted in earlier eras of "being," "doing" and "celebrating" *(koinonia, diakonia, leitourgia)*—emerged as a defining feature of the church and its mission for many mainliners in this decade.

The retrievalist development with the highest cultural visibility in the 1980s was the emergence of the "evangelical empire." Not only in fast-growing "born again" church membership, but also in the publishing field and in the academy, evangelical writers came to increasing prominence. The principal twentieth-century voice of evangelical theology, Carl Henry (completing his six-volume magnum opus),[37] could no longer be ignored by the establishment and was elected president of the American Theological Society. The names of evangelical theologians, such as Donald Bloesch, Millard Erickson, Mark Noll and David Wells, appeared more and more in ecumenical journals. One prominent theologian, Thomas Oden, recanted his earlier liberal views and became a self-designated "paleo-orthodox" evangelical. The highest-profile version of conservative evangelicalism was that of Jerry Falwell and Pat Robertson—the *political* fundamentalism known as the Religious Right. At the same time, evangelical Jim Wallis and his *Sojourners* magazine were urging evangelicalism to the political left. Often perceived as monolithic, evangelicalism was manifestly diverse.

A personal note: I shared Lindbeck's and Frei's concern to retrieve the biblical narrative and worried about its "eclipse," especially in my own denomination, the United Church of Christ. UCC leaders liked to think of themselves as the prophetic vanguard of theology and mission but so often succumbed to the pressures and fashions of the day. In 1984, the year that Lindbeck's *The Nature of Doctrine* was published, the first UCC grassroots Craigville Theological Colloquy was held, recognizing the fiftieth anniversary of the Barmen Declaration. The colloquy had much to teach us about resistance to cultural ideology.

In a "witness statement" I helped write, 170 of us from across the United States echoed Barmen's affirmation of Jesus Christ as our sole Lord. Indeed, the colloquies continue with this commitment. A recent annual gathering posed the question: How can the church be both prophetic *and* catholic? Like other emerging centrist movements in mainline denominations, an offshoot of the colloquies called the "Confessing Christ" movement insistently raises the banner of Barmen.

My writing reflected a concern for Christian foundations for mission in a second systematics volume on the nature of biblical authority[38] and in articles and book chapters on various Christian doctrines. Dot and I worked on many of these same issues for laity in our little volume *Christian Basics.*[39]

As in the first Craigville colloquy, along with the recovery of basic Christian identity we were determined not to forget two things: first, the *context* in which theology is to be done—especially the political, cultural and economic settings; and second, the *conversation* needed among all parts of the body of Christ in order to get the full picture. That meant an appreciation for the past but a refusal to retreat into it. Hence the importance of challenging political fundamentalism in a book, *The Religious Right and Christian Faith,*[40] and a search for new social strategies such as the ministry of laity in the workplace pioneered by the Center for Laity at Andover Newton. Conversation likewise meant listening to the voices of women. With a spouse and a daughter coming into pastoral ministry in the 1980s and another in prison ministry, I could not easily forget this. All of this activity signified a fresh appreciation for the ecumenical movement, especially in its bilateral proposals for "full communion," as in the Lutheran-Reformed Conversation in which I took an active part. It also meant broadening the dialogue to include evangelicals, and with this in mind I wrote extensively on the evangelical-ecumenical conversation.

The 1990s
As the decade is not over, I will attempt no sweeping generalizations; instead, I will indicate three trends and offer some general observations.

The first trend of the 1990s is the increased *tribalizing* of theology—doing theology only in, for and with one's own kind; doing theology *only* from one's own ecclesial traditions—Lutheran, Reformed, Baptist, Anabaptist, Anglican, Methodist, Roman Catholic, Eastern Orthodox, Pentecostal, whatever. Or doing theology only as a member of a camp: process, liberation, liberal, existential, evangelical, evangelical catholic, mystical, modern, postmodern, postliberal, postevangelical, Jesus Seminar and so on. Or doing theology only as an ethnic or gender subcommunity: feminist, womanist, gay and lesbian, African-American, Latin American, North American Hispanic, Asian-American, Native American . . .

A second trend is very different, the erasure of all particularities, not only ethnic, ecclesial and perspectival but also any basic distinction between Christian faith and other world religions and all people of good will. Hence the growth of pluralist theologies based on some common core of truth or holiness (Paul Knitter, John Hick and W. C. Smith, for example, described and demolished so well by Mark Heim in his searching book *Salvations*[41]). Or the relativist version of the same in which no truth claims are made but only a pragmatic theology that "works for me," to use the postmodern pop cliché.

A third development, in its own way more radical than the others, consists not in getting comfortable with one's own tribe or in doing only what "works for me," but in risking encounter with other viewpoints in a "Corinthian model" of theology. Christian theology so construed is a body of truth that requires the contributions of many diverse perspectives (1 Cor 12), engaging one another lovingly (1 Cor 13), and always accountable to Jesus Christ the head of the body. In the same spirit but with a different image—baseball—this kind of approach touches all the bases, not settling for a "single"—a single doctrine, accent, interest or perspective—but attempting to be comprehensive and holistic. At its best, such a development brings together all the accents of the previous decades—*koinonia, diakonia, leitourgia, kerygma.* The latter are, of course, the signs of the Spirit that appeared together in the apostolic church (Acts 2—4)—the full work of the Holy Spirit that marks the faithful church wherever it is found today.

I see this third trend of the 1990s in a resurgence of systematic theology, evidenced by a remarkable number of new, full-scale writing projects dealing with all the Christian doctrines, and by the revival of theology in seminaries and pastors' study groups. I see it in the bilateral and multilateral proposals for full communion and covenant. I see it in the developing evangelical-ecumenical conversation and comradeship. I see it in the growing centrist movements. In all cases, two refrains are discernible: (1) a commitment to deal with the Great Tradition and its biblical foundations and (2) a determination to bring the Christian faith into living relationship to this time and place.

A final personal note: It's not hard to discern which of these developments strike fire with the Fackres. I researched the systematics revival for a presidential address to the American Theological Society in 1991, have chronicled it in recent articles, and have tried to practice it in my own developing seven-volume systematics.[42] I have been deeply involved in the growing evangelical-ecumenical partnership, the new and more modest bilateral ecumenism, and the neoconfessing centrist movement, all grounded in loyalty to the Center and the centralities as they relate to the claims of Jesus Christ for today.

There is much to be learned from the past fifty years of theology, mission and ministry. The hardest lesson of all has to do with the seductability of the church to current fashions and our forgetfulness about the *durable* goods of the gospel. The Good News is always and everywhere the Good News, having to do with the triune God who brought the world into being, raised up Israel, came among us in Jesus Christ, conquered sin and death, reconciled the world, gave birth to the church, poured out salvation, and will finally bring the full reign of God. Theology must continually return to this overarching Story, this perduring structure of Christian teaching with its "one foundation . . . Jesus Christ." Yes, let it relate ever and again to new times and places. As Pastor John Robinson of Pilgrim days reminded us, "ever-new light and truth shall break forth from God's holy Word." Yes, relate to the changing scene, but do not succumb to its premises. Yes, answer its questions, but also question its answers. Listen to the one Word, Jesus Christ, the same yesterday, today and forever. Without the durable, theology indeed becomes ephemeral.

Part II
Signs of Recentering

End-of-century theology and church life, while diverse, show signs of a turn to "the center." This section opens with an overview of centrist developments in mainline churches, movements that resist the left/right culture wars in both society and church, returning to classical Christian centralities. The section continues with chapters on the recovery of foundational teaching in both local churches and seminaries, and concludes with chapters on two neglected Christian doctrines—eschatology and angelology—ones that speak to popular ideologies of the day.

2

The Church
of the Center†

H. RICHARD NIEBUHR'S INFLUENTIAL *CHRIST AND CULTURE* IS REMEMBERED
for its thoughtful delineation of five types of church/culture encounter.
Often forgotten is Niebuhr's discernment of a "church of the center"
within this pattern.[1] The description of that constituency in its historic
form anticipates by four decades self-conscious efforts to "re-form" an
ecclesial and theological *center* in North American Protestantism.

Commentaries on the emerging center abound, as in a spate of
Christian Century articles: "Evangelical and Ecumenical: Re-forming
the Center"; "Forming an Emphatic Christian Center"; "What Culture
War? The View From the Center"; "When the Denominational Center
Doesn't Hold: The Southern Baptist Experience."[2] Since 1992, a major
research project, "Re-forming the Center," has been under way,
conceived by Douglas Jacobsen and William Trollinger Jr. of Messiah
College, arguing for a centrist alternative to the influential left-right
"culture-war" analysis.[3] Jack Rogers believes that 75 percent of

† This essay was based on an article of the same name for the issue of *Interpretation* on the centrist
phenomenon in mainline churches, vol. 51 (April 1997): 130-42.

American Protestantism is of this mind. In *Claiming the Center* he declares:

> If mainstream denominations will return to playing their appropriate role, they can provide a needed balance between those more one-sided groups to the left and the right.[4]

Just what is this ecclesial, theological and ethical center? Detractors have characterized it as "the mushy middle" and "the muddled middle." In the pithy words of Texan John Nance Garner, former U.S. vice president: "Ain't nothin in the middle uh the road but yeller lines and dead armadillers!" Defenders, on the other hand, declare it to be an "emphatic middle," even a "radical middle." Still others view it less as a constituency and more as a safe space for conversation among disputants, a "middle ground" or "common ground." In this overview we examine the increasingly self-conscious mainline Protestant "center," with learnings from Niebuhr's early taxonomy and critiques of it, together with a case study of one centrist development. So framed, its defining characteristics, tensions and prospects begin to emerge.

Christ, Culture and Center

In *Christ and Culture,* H. Richard Niebuhr's types are bounded at the left end by the "Christ *against* culture" and on the right by the "Christ *of* culture."[5] The *church of the center* is composed of a threesome: "Christ above culture," "Christ and culture in paradox," and "Christ transformer of culture." How so a "center"? Niebuhr believes that

> the great majority movement in Christianity, which we may call the church of the center, has refused to take either the position of the anticultural radicals or that of the accommodation of Christ to culture. Yet it has not regarded its efforts at solution of the Christ-culture problem as compromising . . . for its fundamental issue does not lie between Christ and the world, important as that issue is, but between God and [humanity]. The Christ-culture problem is approached from this point of view and with this conviction. Hence, wide as are the divergences among various groups in the church of the center they agree on certain points when they ask about their responsibility in the social life. The agreement is formulated in *theological* terms. The relevance of

such formulae to practical questions is often obscure both to radical critics and to uncritical followers.[6]

Two features of the church of the center emerge in this description. One is the obvious point suggested by the use of the metaphor: a center constituency falls between right and left. It rejects the reduction of the dynamic between Christ and culture to one or other extreme. With regard to Niebuhr's problematic, the church neither accommodates to, nor flees from, the culture around it. In a larger sense, on any matter of ecclesiology or theology, the center resists reductionism. At the same time, it attempts to honor the *legitimate* accents of polar partisans, bringing them into fruitful interrelationship.

A second feature of the center is its focus on *theology*. Theology, in the sense of Niebuhr's God-world relationship, is the attempt to hold the church accountable to its own self-defined identity, resisting thereby both a chameleonlike adaptation to culture and a kneejerk rejection of it, the proculture conservative captivity and the anticulture radical dismissal. The Christian community so constituted has recourse to its own theological standards for making decisions about Christ/culture relations, albeit with varying interpretations, as in the three historic types that constitute the "church of the center."

Niebuhr's analysis purports to be descriptive. However, the characterizations of each type show his normative sympathies for the threefold center, and in particular, the "Christ transforming culture" version of it.

This typology has its critics. Although no public evidence exists,[7] a case can be made that Reinhold Niebuhr took issue with his brother's characterizations, both descriptively and normatively. Critic Niebuhr was fond of saying that the gospel frees one to move "theologically to the right and politically to the left." Indeed, he took that unpredictable course in his own journey, regularly eluding theological and political typecasting.[8] Both his contention and his practice suggest another kind of centering, a focus on an orientation point beyond the conventional options, making for unpredictable mobility among them. So conceived, the center is not a middle between two extremes, as in H. Richard's threefold constituency. Rather, it has to do with a Center who prompts the unconventional move. Such a commitment to Jesus Christ makes for the freedom to say a firm yes to the left or right as the occasion demands and the Center requires, rather than a predictable yes and no to each. H. Richard's center stresses the "both-and"; Reinhold's stresses the "either-or." The former inclines toward irenics, the latter toward polemics.[9]

Dietrich Bonhoeffer also made use of the imagery in question, particularly in his work *Christ the Center.*[10] Absolute loyalty to Jesus Christ meant for him the relativizing of all human partisanships, freedom *from* regnant ideologies and freedom *for* risk-taking options. Karl Barth struck the same note in the 1934 Barmen Declaration of the Confessing Church, in its opposition to German blood-and-soil philosophy:

> Jesus Christ, as he is attested for us in Holy Scripture, is the one Word of God which we have to hear and which we have to obey in life and in death. We reject the false doctrine, as though the Church could and would have to acknowledge as a source of its proclamation, apart from and beside the one Word of God, still other events and powers, figures and truths. as God's revelation.[11]

This kind of center/Center is worlds away from a modulated "middle way" and a "mushy middle." As Jack Rogers observes,

> The center is not just a passive midpoint between extremes to the right and the left. It is a substantive core of conviction.[12]

H. Richard Niebuhr's pinpointing of a historic church of the center puts us on the track of a similar phenomenon in the late twentieth century. Especially helpful is his identification of two of its key features: its resistance to culture-driven left-right polarities and its concern for theological identity. But the emerging centrist phenomenon also reflects Reinhold Niebuhr's caveat, and its echoes in the confession and action of Bonhoeffer and Barth: a center whose loyalty is solely to Christ the Center and as such not bound to "the middle way," or to cultural categories and continuums.

But is not the concept "center" itself a cultural category, indeed part of a political continuum of "left," "center," "right"? Does not the very use of such a secular notion violate the call to listen only to the one Word, Jesus Christ, and not to other "events, powers, figures and truths"?

The issue of the church's appropriation of cultural idiom was posed very early in its encounter with the *logos* philosophies of the ancient world. In the Johannine writings and subsequent patristic traditions, the term and concept *logos* was confronted, converted and baptized. Resisting the "anticultural radicals," classical Christian thought appropriated it, but, rejecting the cultural accommodationists, transformed its meaning. Thus an early mainstream Christian tradition exemplified the centrist orientation and showed how categories from culture can be adopted and transformed by their new christological matrix. The Niebuhr brothers' exchange is itself a replay of appropriation/conversion aspects of cultural encounter. H. Richard Niebuhr's employment of the concept is in continuity with its use as a middle term in a political spectrum, while the centering of Reinhold Niebuhr-cum-Bonhoeffer and Barth stress departure from cultural expectations.

The United Church of Christ: A Quest for the Center
The United Church of Christ, often thought to be at the left end of the mainline Protestant spectrum, is a showcase of the late twentieth-century struggle for a "church of the center." A survey of recent developments within this church may thus illustrate the defining characteristics of the new-but-old centrist phenomenon.

In 1980 a *Time* magazine story, "A Pallid but Personable Faith," commented on a study of mainline Protestantism, one that found the United Church of Christ "noteworthy in how little interest its members displayed concerning a pastor's religiosity, biblical faith, evangelism, piety or explicit emphasis on spiritual renewal and liturgy."[13] Aware of the increasingly culture-driven trends in their church, a group of UCC pastors organized a 1984 grassroots colloquy to celebrate the fiftieth anniversary of the Barmen Declaration, viewing the anniversary as an occasion for a current declaration of theological independence from cultural ideologies. What does it mean to say *now*, as Barmen said *then*, that we must listen only to "the one Word of God . . . Jesus Christ as he is attested for us in Holy Scripture"?

One hundred and seventy pastors and laity from around the country gathered on the UCC's Craigville, Massachusetts, conference

grounds for the anniversary, and after intense exchanges about the
state of the church declared in a "witness statement":

> With Barmen we confess fidelity to "the one Word of God which
> we have to hear, . . . trust and obey in life and in death. *Christ is
> the Center* to whom we turn in the midst of the clamors, uncer-
> tainties and temptations of the hour. . . . We acknowledge our own
> part in the confusions and captivities of the times. The trumpet
> has too often given an uncertain sound . . . our words have often
> not been God's Word, and our deeds have often been timid and
> trivial. Where theological disarray and lackluster witness are our
> lot, it is "our own fault, our own most grievous fault."[14]

The Statement set forth *affirmations* that give the church its theological
identity—the Christian story from creation to consummation, with its
centerpoint in Jesus Christ; the authority of Scripture; the resource role
of the classical tradition; the inclusivity and catholicity of the church;
and the call to the struggle for justice and peace. It added to the
affirmations a list of *rejections,* citing in the words of Barmen, ideologies
of

> the right or the left, as though the Church were permitted to
> abandon . . . its message . . . to changes in prevailing ideological
> and political convictions. (Barmen 8:18)

The wire services took note of the meeting, reporting it as a break-
through for a denomination perceived as a weathervane of the
cultural *Zeitgeist* and a church not known for its theological interests.

These grassroots colloquies have continued annually, each year
taking up critical issues such as the authority and interpretation of
Scripture, Christology in a pluralist world, the doctrine of the Holy
Spirit, the sacraments and ministry, the meaning of salvation, the
mission of the church and the trinitarian formula for baptism. The
history of the colloquies is a study in the three stigmata of "the church
of the center" discernible in the Niebuhr brothers' analysis and
exchange.

The Center as Span
The first feature of the center is its role as a *bridge* over the chasm
between right and left. The title of the 1996 colloquy reflected exactly
that function, with the background of sharp partisanships in the

mainline churches: "How Can the Church Be Both Prophetic and Catholic?" In the years since their inception, these gatherings have become, according to a reporter in *United Church News,* the principal theological forum in the United Church of Christ. The church of the center as "span" entails providing a safe space where otherwise hostile partisans can cross culture-war boundaries and speak to one another. Here is the center as "common ground," a "center that doesn't exclude," a "multivoiced center," "a center of friends" as described in a paper prepared by Douglas Jacobsen and William Trollinger Jr. for the 1996 conference of the project called "Re-forming the Center."[15] Indeed, the research in this project has uncovered much nineteenth- and twentieth-century evidence that the church has not been driven by cultural orthodoxies, nor has it regularly succumbed to its left-right wars. Nor must it do so today.

In its spanning role, the church of the center provides an important alternative to the developing tribalism in both church and society, one in which each constituency more and more hunkers down on its own turf, speaking its distinctive language to its own people, defining rigorously and defending determinedly its own boundaries. The rise of ecclesial tribalisms cries out for a witness to catholicity. Honor the diversity, but attend as well to the Pauline counsel: "the eye cannot say to the hand, 'I have no need of you'" (1 Cor 12:21). A bridge-building center constitutes a meeting ground for civil conversation among disputants. Here diversity is understood as charisms reaching out to one another, seeking a fuller body of Christ.

The church of the center in its bridge-building role, while an alternative to ecclesial war-making, does not gloss over differences. Bridge talk includes mutual *admonition* as well as mutual affirmation, the formula ventured by the recent North American Lutheran-Reformed dialogue.[16] The eye has every right to remind the hand that "standing" alone, a hand is an odd-looking body. And vice versa. As such, the invitation to mutual fructification is a model of diversity juxtaposed to the currently popular "theological pluralism." In the latter case, a plea is made to recognize the equal legitimacy of alternative understandings of the Christian faith, in popular lingo, "different strokes for different folks . . . you do your thing and I'll do mine." Theological pluralism, so understood, is a justification of the status quo. Paul's Corinthian catholicity rejects this static view, demanding an interactive diversity, one in which the "variety of gifts" are engaged in a demanding mutual encounter, learning and growing into and as the body of Christ.

The center as span is grounded deeply in classical theological commitments, especially in the doctrine of the Trinity. The triune God as Three-in-One affirms the diversity and distinctions of Father, Son and Holy Spirit in a *perichoretic* unity. In this "coinherence," God is not just loving; God *is* Love—Mutuality, Community, Sociality, Life Together.[17] And who God is constitutes what God wills for the world: community, *shalom*, a life together in freedom and peace. The church, the body of Christ on earth, is thus called with its many parts to live and work in a mutually enriching ecclesial koinonia—a church of the center performing its "bridge-work."

The Center and the Centralities

A second feature of the colloquies reflects H. Richard Niebuhr's accent on the *theological* role of the center. Whatever the question, the church is called to approach it on its own theological terms. Contrary to the slogan of another day—"let the world set the agenda"—the church sets its own agenda, carefully reads the minutes of its prior meetings, speaks its own language, and draws on its own rich lore. Let the church be the church! Or in the refrain of a "postliberal" theology: the world of the Bible must absorb the extrabiblical world, not the other way around. (Interestingly, 1984 was the date of both the first Craigville Colloquy and the publication of George Lindbeck's groundbreaking work *The Nature of Doctrine.*)[18]

To retrieve the specifics of Christian theology and to reinterrogate the classical Christian tradition for its relevance today have been continuing features of the colloquies. A centrist movement strives to reclaim the *centralities*, the "commonplaces," the classical *loci* of Christian teaching. Without clear theological guidelines, preaching, teaching, counseling, administrating, organizing, ministry, mission and even our music take their signals from the culture (and the culture wars) around us. The Craigville Colloquies have thus unabashedly given pride of place to central Christian doctrines—Christology, Trinity, soteriology, theological epistemology . . . With the popular self-designation of the

UCC as the "just peace church" in mind, the colloquies were a witness to theology grounding the social witness, rather than, as is too often the case, the social-action agenda driving the theology.

The reframing of issues theologically has its counterpart elsewhere in today's mainline institutions. One sign of it is a retrieval of the classical teaching in seminary theology departments and a surge in the writing of systematic theology. Within the past twenty years, almost seventy full-scale projects covering all the standard loci—from single volumes to seven-volume series—have been published in English.[19] The same concern for foundational teaching is taking place in congregations, as evidenced in the laity's fresh interest in "the basics," the emphasis in mainline congregations on preaching and worship, and the widespread use of the lectionary by pastors and congregations in both preaching and teaching.

Center spanning and theological centering—the first two marks of the church of the center—are inseparable. Indeed they were inextricable in the earliest Christian communities: the Acts 2—4 partnership of *kerygma, leitourgia, koinonia* and *diakonia.* Conversation on the center span requires a common language and lore. We must attend to the cultural *context,* but do so with our own *texts*— Scripture and tradition—and with the theological frameworks of the Christian community.

Christ the Center

A third feature of the center is pointed to in the Reinhold Niebuhr proviso. We see it played out in a turn taken in the history of the Craigville Colloquies.

Colloquy 1 had a cross-section of people and perspectives, but the Barmen anniversary tended to attract folk who were deeply troubled by a regnant culture-Protestantism. They wanted to say a clear word about this captivity, just as the Confessing Church in Germany of the 1930s had said it in its own time and place. Its Witness Statement, with both *affirmations* and *rejections,* did just that. But then something happened.

The high visibility of the first colloquy began to attract an even wider range of views. While the next four colloquies were able to produce a common declaration on Scripture, baptism, Eucharist and ministry, the widening circle of conversation changed the character of the final document of each colloquy; there was no longer a unified witness. Initially, this consisted in the citing of consensus where it occurred, but also the noting of secondary areas of disagreement. Later, it meant only a listing of "agreements and disagreements" (the colloquy on abortion), then the substitution of a paper written by an editorial committee seeking to capture the flavor of the small group discussions for the earlier "witness statements," and finally, a published paper consisting only of reports from the many small groups on their week-long conversations and conclusions. The countercultural Barmen-like note struck in the first colloquy receded, as polemics gave way to irenics.

In 1993, at Colloquy 10, with the subject "Theological Standards for Ministry in the United Church of Christ," a reaction set in. Yes, dialogue, yes, theology, but what of fidelity to the "one Word, Jesus Christ"? For some of the participants, the two-point centrism of the current colloquies—bridge-building and focus on theology—was proving "necessary, but not sufficient." One small group report, after expressing approval of the theological standards stated in the UCC ordination rite—confession of Christ as Lord and Savior, biblical authority, loyalty to the classical Christian tradition, all to be faithfully lived out in the contemporary context—questioned whether such commitments were alive and well in UCC congregations and in the denomination. Many at the colloquy had been reading Leander Keck's Beecher lectures, *The Church Confident,* with its indictment of mainline churches for their obeisance to the therapeutic, relativist and politically correct ideologies of the day.[20] But these same folk, committed to bridge-building, had not joined the denomination-bashing and schismatic mood growing in mainline Protestantism, as represented by many self-styled "biblical renewal" movements. What to do?

The "Confessing Christ" movement in the UCC was born from the concerns expressed at the tenth colloquy. It brought to the fore the *third* feature of "the church of the center": the unambiguous call for sole loyalty to the one Center. The invitation letter from fifteen pastors and teachers to a list of 450 people thought to be interested put it this way:

We believe the future of our Church depends on faithfulness to the one Word of the triune God, Jesus Christ, whom we are "to hear and which we are to trust and obey in life and in death." . . . We are deeply concerned . . . that the commitment to "listen for God's Word in Holy Scripture" and "in our rich theological heritage" is often neglected in our Church. We view this indifference to Scripture and debilitating amnesia as a threat to the Gospel. . . . We believe we here give voice to the concerns of the *often-silent center* of our Church. . . . The time has come . . . for thoughtful, joyous and imaginative theological work that undergirds our defining [social action and cultural] commitments. To that end we invite you to join us in dialogue about the meaning and importance of that heritage. We envision continuing conversation . . . where we can *reaffirm* this faith, *reclaim* its biblical roots, *retrieve* its historic resources, and think together about the controverted questions within our Church and the culture.[21]

All three center notes are struck here: conversation across the span on the disputed questions, a theological framework for the discourse, and at the heart of the invitation, an unqualified commitment to the "one Word, Jesus Christ." The latter is underlined in the very name of the movement, *Confessing Christ.*

How this third factor has pressed Confessing Christ to supplement the Craigville colloquies returns us to trinitarian terms. The Trinity as Community is a theological basis for the *span* mandate, the first centrist principle. But the Second Person of the Trinity is the Word incarnate, the One disclosing who the triune God is and what the triune God wills. As such, the Trinity is not a broad warrant for any kind of "togetherness" in the church, but rather for a church that is "not conformed to this world but transformed" by, and faithful to, Jesus Christ. Here is a *tough* love, a *holy* love (P. T. Forsyth), able to say a no as well as a yes, ready to risk polemics as well as venture irenics.

A remarkable response came to the invitation letter: four hundred pastors appeared at three regional meetings held around the country. In the years since, a Statement of Purpose has been set forth based on the UCC's theological Preamble to its Constitution, asserting the centrality of Christ, the primacy of Scripture, the role of creeds and Christian tradition, yet the need to make this faith "our own" in ever-new contexts, as exemplified in the UCC Statement of Faith's call for "courage in the struggle for justice and peace." Many workshops, research projects and missions have taken place with several thousand clergy and laity participating. A daily prayer, creed and lection discipline developed, a newsletter was published, and a vigorous Ecunet meeting was launched with over six thousand notes from both supporters and critics of the Confessing Christ movement. An Internet website was set up, and another theological dialogue developed among those committed to centrist purposes. Various booklets have been produced on current theological issues and a major book has been published, *How Shall We Sing the Lord's Song?* critiquing *The New Century Hymnal.* Seven regional "centers" have emerged, one on a northeastern conference grounds, another at a midwestern college, and the rest housed in congregations. A major long-range project has been undertaken, the writing of a catechism for UCC congregations. Current theological developments have been the focus of regional consultations that have focused on current theological developments, such as the 1993 Re-Imagining Conference, the Jesus Seminar, religious pluralism, inclusive language, same-sex unions and issues in new hymnody. Seminars have been held on preaching the church year and on Christian basics for laity. Research is currently being done on the church's mission with the working poor and a theological response to genetic engineering. A national steering committee of twenty—convened under UCC Wisconsin Conference Minister Frederick Trost—gathers twice a year and is otherwise in touch by conference call. All of this occurs on a budget from personal contributions of barely $10,000 a year.

The centrist ferment in the United Church of Christ has its counterparts elsewhere, varying in issues, accents, strength and strategies. The group SEAD (Scholarly Engagement with Anglican Doctrine) and the volume *Reclaiming the Faith* strike notes similar to Confessing Christ. The 1990-1992 "Call to Faithfulness" Conferences, the Center for Catholic and Evangelical Theology, the journal *Rose* and the 9.5 movement in very different ways represent a neoconfessional expression of the center in the Evangelical Lutheran Church of America. The United Methodist "Confessing Church" movement brings together self-identified evangelicals and centrists. The center may emerge as a common sensibility and direction, rather than in an organized form, as is described in Rogers's *Claiming the Center* in the PC (U.S.A.), or in the recent appeal of former American Baptist leaders for respite from and a nonpolarized approach to the culture wars around issues of homosexuality.[22] Transdenominational expressions of a centrist constituency and concern include the study project "Re-forming the Center" earlier noted, and the "Gospel and Culture Network" that took rise in this country from the writings and influence of Lesslie Newbigin.[23]

While there is an identifiable center reforming in mainline Protestantism, it is a fragile and still diverse phenomenon, with fragility and diversity interrelated. Each of the three features of the center has its advocates: those that stress the (1) bridging, (2) theological or (3) polemical aspects, with 2 assimilable to either 1 or 3. These tensions play out regularly in Confessing Christ. Do we hold a consultation on a current theological question with all sides represented equally in the conversation and no Confessing Christ position taken? Or do we engage in unambiguous defense of a point of view on controverted questions such as the trinitarian formula for baptism, the Jesus Seminar or the rise of the pluralist theologies? Do we take up only theological issues or also show their implication for culture, especially with the UCC's justice and peace commitments in mind? Do we take strong stands against questionable theological and cultural positions of the denomination or provide only a needed forum for combatants? Other movements in mainline churches, associated either with conservative evangelicalism on the one hand or with liberal Protestantism on the other, are not troubled by these kinds of questions.

The attempt to hold the three characteristics together is reflected in the Confessing Christ response to the current *New Century Hymnal* controversy in the UCC, a case study within a case study of the emerging center.

The Center and *The New Century Hymnal*
The name of the new 1995 hymnal reflects the intention of its compilers—an agency in the United Church of Christ known as the United Church Board for Homeland Ministries: anticipate the world of

tomorrow—a world religiously and ethnically pluralist—and a faith
that is pluralist, nonchauvinist, pacific, nonhierarchical, inclusive
. . . reworking the language of inherited hymnody to fit this *new
century,* avoiding all hesitations of other new purportedly inclusivist
hymnbooks whose compromises lock them into the assumptions of
the "old" twentieth century.

The publication of the hymnal prompted a story in the February
12, 1996, *Newsweek.* The religion editor, Kenneth Woodward, took
delight in quoting the new version of "America the Beautiful." *TNCH*
revisers, detecting imperialism, changed the hymn throughout,
eliminating the theme "O beautiful for patriot dream . . . America,
America . . ." and substituting "How beautiful two continents . . .
Americas, Americas . . ." Woodward noted also the disappearance of
"Father, Son and Holy Spirit" and other language deemed offensive—
such as "darkness" and "blindness"—the appearance of a "Father-
Mother" deity, the "neutering" of Jesus (no masculine pronouns
permitted), the "above" imagery of heaven horizontalized, and so
forth. Hymnal critic Willis Elliott was quoted as charging "the advent
of a new religion." The article also stated that "many members" of
the United Church of Christ plan to "air their complaints at a meeting
in Boylston, Massachusetts next April." The story evoked a storm of
criticism of the hymnal from *Newsweek* readers. On the other hand,
its supporters were outraged by the article, attacking Woodward's
treatment of the subject and Elliott's views.[24]

The production and defense of a hymnbook different from all
others in its responsiveness to cultural developments, and the attack
on it by angry critics, illustrate today's left-right culture wars making
their way into North American church life. But contrary to the
Newsweek description, the Boylston gathering was not sponsored by
presumed right-wing forces viewing all change as repugnant, but by
the centrist Confessing Christ movement. Many of Confessing
Christ's participants affirm the importance of "inclusive language"
but know that there are a variety of interpretations of its meaning
(eleven at least—from the modest changing of language for humanity to the bolder use of *Goddess* in tandem with *God* or the elimination
of all reference to deity as intrinsically hierarchical).[25] Offering
themselves as the meaning of hymnic inclusivity, innocent of the

range of views on the subject, *The New Century Hymnal* alterations required a response.

Confessing Christ had held an earlier meeting based on a small published *TNCH* "sampler," inviting both critic Willis Elliott and the chair of the hymnal committee to present their cases. (The hymnal was embargoed until publication in the summer of 1995, sight unseen by all including those who purchased it for their congregations at reduced prepublication cost.) Since its publication, the hymnal has been vigorously promoted, ecumenically as well as denominationally. The Boylston meeting was called as a forum to explore its theological premises. Yes, the voice of the UCC critics, silent in official circles, would be heard from; but also, an invitation would be extended to the hymnal's producers and advocates to respond.

A UCC church historian made a presentation at Boylston, acknowledging the strengths of the hymnal—the introduction of the psalter, hymns from other ethnic and ecclesial traditions, biographical notes—but pressed the tough theological questions: how are the hymnic substitutes for God as "Father, Son and Holy Spirit," such as "God, Christ, Spirit" or "Creator, Redeemer, Sanctifier," not Arian? (In the first instance, only the first person is God, and in the second, the *doing* of God in the "economy" is substituted for the *being* of God—the "ontology," Christ becoming a creature of the Creator.) Is not a subordinationist Trinity of this sort—one that abandons the traditional coequality of the persons—a bad model and mandate for the UCC's concern about justice and equality? How is the removal of Jesus' full humanity (no masculine pronouns permitted) not Docetism? What happens to the divine sovereignty when the word *Lord* is removed from the hymnal in references to God and the divinity of Christ? (It was restored in some references to the humanity of Jesus after a 1994 General Synod challenged the planned removal of every appearance of *Lord* in old hymns and new.) How the committee arrived at its theological decisions was also taken up in a presentation by one of the hymnal committee members who had, with two other members, resigned in protest over the developing viewpoints, seen by them as the agenda of the denominational agency rather than the will of the UCC constituency.

Confrontation was there at Boylston. But so was the effort at conversation. The head of the agency that published *The New Century Hymnal* was invited, and he sent three representatives for a panel response. The chair of the hymnal committee, its editor and other supporters were also on hand with much literature. Small groups met and many viewpoints were expressed. The lively meeting of 130 folk from across the country provided material for a Confessing Christ theological critique of the hymnal *How Shall We Sing the Lord's Song?*[26] The Confessing Christ leadership views the hymnal as a teaching moment for the UCC on matters of theological identity and integrity.

The role of Confessing Christ in the hymnbook controversy reflects all three aspects of the reforming center: a center span for conversation across the left-right divide, the theological terms for discourse on this bridge, and a christological norm that frees centrists for polemics as well as irenics.

Prospects
Does the *center* have a future—either in organized form as in Confessing Christ or other comparable movements, or in making its presence felt and voice heard in other ways?

The Center and the Mainline
One current scenario of the future of mainline Protestantism is the continuing breakup of denominations as we now know them. Some see a return to the congregation and the demise of national churches—a new localism. Others project a minimal survival of denominations based on their restructuring as a servicing agency for congregations. Yet others predict the continuance in some form of national church bodies, but their reconfiguration.

Centrist movements and mindsets share in the erosion of confidence in national offices, insofar as the latter succumb to cultural orthodoxies. The church of the center could contribute to any or all of these possibilities. However, the grounding of the present mainline churches in classical texts and the participation of some denominational leaders in centrist movements (four of the thirty-nine regional UCC Conference Ministers were among the signatories of the original Confessing Christ letter) militate against the new local-isms. Further, as Tony Campolo has argued, mainline denominations, or something like them, are needed as carriers of classical Christian identity, especially vis-à-vis "lone ranger" megachurches led by flamboyant personalities easily vulnerable to cultural seductions.[27] Nevertheless, the lack of trust in denominational leadership and its programs is pervasive. Further, centrists are finding each other across denominational lines. But these movements are still fragile, so it is too early to forecast what role the church of the center will play in any of these scenarios.

The Center and Ecumenism

The day of denominational mergers is, for the time being, over. Ambitious plans made in utopian times have been significantly scaled back. COCU, the North American Consultation on Church Union, child of the ecumenically exuberant 1960s, earlier projected a union of nine major mainline denominations. In 1984 (1984 again!) it altered course from a union of denominations to a "communion of churches" *(communio)*, proposing a "covenanting" process to achieve the more modest goal of reconciled ministries, eucharistic hospitality, and joint plans for mission.[28] Nevertheless, COCU and a number of "bilateral" dialogues have achieved significant *theological* advances, as in the *COCU Consensus,* the Lutheran-Reformed European *Leuenberg Concord,* the North American *Invitation to Action* and *Common Calling,* and the North American Lutheran-Episcopal *Concordat.* They have done so by careful attention to the classical texts of the historic traditions. Behind these are major ecumenical doctrinal achievements, from the WCC's *Baptism, Eucharist and Ministry* and its six volumes of official responses from national churches around the world, to its more recent *Confessing the Apostolic Faith* based on the Nicene Creed.

The historic creeds, confessions and traditions on which these discussions and their agreements are based are, for the most part, the same ones to which the center movements appeal. A significant convergence appears, therefore, in the agendas of ecumenists and centrists. Indeed, the leadership in pressing the ecumenical case in a given denomination often overlaps with the leadership in the centrist movement within that same denomination.[29] Might this convergence be reflected ecclesially? For example, after a bilateral or multilateral vote or declaration (1997 and 2001 being key years, respectively, for the Lutheran/Reformed, Lutheran/Episcopal and COCU decisions) will a Presbyterian congregation discover ties that bind it to local Lutheran and UCC congregations because of common centrist commitments? Already there is evidence for these kinships in cyberspace where new technology enables people of the center (as well as those on the left and right) to overleap conventional boundaries.[30]

The Center and Evangelicalism

An impressive evangelical-ecumenical conversation is current, as in the 1995 Wheaton College conference that brought together "evangelicals and postliberals" with the publication of some of its papers in *The Nature of Confession*.[31] Confessing Christ is itself another example of this convergence. "Evangelical ecumenicals" and "ecumenical evangelicals" find themselves regularly together in the struggles of "the church of the center." They share a core of theological centralities, a common commitment to Jesus Christ rather than cultural ideology, and the bridge-building *ecumenical* adjective or noun.[32]

Where will this new colleagueship finally go? Certainly in ad hoc ventures and countless other consultations, in book projects, informal contacts, and comradeship in social justice struggles and cultural causes. And to the degree that it becomes institutionalized in centrist movements, possibly much more. But the jury is, again, still out.

Hopes

The "center," as described here, intrinsically resists fissiparation. But at its own heart there is a certain diversity. It has constituencies that gravitate toward one or another of its three defining characteristics. The church of the center is a risky mix, even an improbable one. Indeed, the first and third qualities almost seem poised to oppose one other: the tender-hearted *both/and* bridgework of the center span, and the tough-minded *either/or* of allegiance alone to Christ the Center.

For all its internal diversity, the center, by definition, is set against reductionism, in particular the reductionism of left or right. Hope for its future requires the maintenance of its full-orbed character, never reducing its witness to any one of its essentials. Standing alone, the center as span flirts with an uncritical "you-all-come" pluralism with no theological norms and no capacity for a clear yes to Jesus Christ and no to untruth. Standing alone, a fix on the theological centralities invites the degeneration of the center into a theological debating society with no commitment to either the issues of the day or the capacity for a bold theological yes that carries with it a bold theological no. Standing alone, the focus on Christ as Center can fall back into the "us and them" mentality that it resists in the culture warriors of the right and left, having no place for the necessary bridgework. The centerline is a tightrope walk.

Two other obvious hopes are the fructification of the "church of the center" by ecumenism and evangelicalism, which feed the church of the center and in turn are fed by it. Indeed, the mainline churches would serve themselves well by encouraging just these coalitions in their own ranks. Such a "life together" points to even a larger hope, one we pray for daily in our Confessing Christ discipline: the health and faithfulness of the church universal. The church of the *center* at its best is a steward of a vision of the wholeness of the church, the church of the *circumference,* the one, holy, catholic and apostolic church. May the need of having a "church of the center" pass away with the coming of a church catholic, in which the eye no longer says to the hand "I have no need of you," and all the members of that body—on its right side and on its left—acknowledge the one Head, Jesus Christ.

3

Centralities
in the Parish[†]

THE NEW CHRISTIAN EDUCATOR AT SOUTH CHURCH, THE CONGREGATION IN
which I hold membership, caused a small stir . . . even before
beginning. It was the credentials. Wheaton College? Why would a
250-year-old mainline church get someone from an evangelical
tradition?

JS has been on site now for two years and we are all cheering,
including the skeptics. Why so?

The predictable answer from some will be: "Church school now
is more than crayons and cookies. The kids learn Bible stories." No.
Scripture had never departed South Church—from the pastor's lectionary children's sermons to the classroom curricula. Something
else is going on here. It has to do with new attention to the big *Story*
within the biblical stories, the *content* within the method and materials. South Church's Christian educator has taken her place in a line
of teachers that winds its way back to Clement of Alexandria, Gregory

---

[†]This essay was first published as "The Commonplaces of Christian Education" in *Christian
Education Journal* 15 (Spring 1995): 27-37.

Thaumaturgus and Cyril of Jerusalem.[1] Using whatever ways of communication prove helpful, she sees her task as the introduction of those she serves to the *defining narrative* of Christian faith.

This development in the educational mission of our congregation reflects the quest for "re-centering" current in mainline Protestantism. "What is it then that *we* believe?" ask the parishioners who see on television's "Oprah" and "Jerry Springer" the protagonists of reincarnation, the devotees of Satan worship, those on friendly terms with angels, the followers of Hare Krishna, the acolytes of Sun Moon . . . and passionate fundamentalists who consign all the foregoing to hell. So too, the questions parishioners bring to pastors and teachers in this pluralistic society: How can we say Jesus Christ is "the way, the truth and the life" when our neighbors who go to the synagogue seem to be better people than some of the members of our own church? Or when the devout Buddhist monk and the ardent Muslim cleric are so convinced that they, not we, are right?

The search for Christian identity goes on apace in establishment churches, especially now among those who for so long took foundational matters for granted and went on to focus on service to human need, to develop a supportive life together, to work for institutional growth, to quest for a deeper spirituality. Now, a too-long bashful *kerygma* becomes bolder, making its way to partnership with these other marks of the church—*diakonia, koinonia* and *leitourgia.* And the articulation of the gospel is taking shape, as in South Church, in *didache,* the teaching ministry. Indeed, it's no coincidence that in my own denomination, the United Church of Christ, a grassroots movement has begun to develop a "catechism" for its children (in conjunction with similar efforts today in European Christianity). This activist church—the UCC—is getting worried about the next generation suffering theological amnesia and losing the very rationale that has driven it into social mission.[2]

Throughout mainline Protestantism much soul-searching now goes on about the erosion of theological foundations. New Testament scholar and former Yale Divinity School dean Leander Keck gives voice to these concerns in his widely read 1992 Beecher Lectures, *The Church Confident: Christianity Can Repent but It Must Not Whimper.*[3] A similar critique emerges in the seven-volume internal study of the Presbyterian Church, U.S.A.[4] And even evangelicalism, so long known for its doctrinal commitments, is being charged by its own leaders with cultural captivity, the vacuity of its preaching and teaching, and the loss of theological substance. So argues David Wells argues in his groundbreaking *No Place for Truth: Whatever Happened to Evangelical Theology?*[5]

Response to this theological depletion has begun to appear in seminary theology departments, a sector of "Christian education." Research in the teaching of theology shows that *retrieval* of the classical tradition is an increasingly prominent factor in schools around the country.[6] Another related phenomenon is the remarkable surge in the writing of works in systematic theology which revisit all the historic benchmarks of Christian belief. In the last twenty years, over seventy such projects have been launched, in sharp contrast to the relative absence of full-scale systematics since the days of such giants as Barth, Brunner and Tillich.[7]

The systematics discipline and current developments within it provide a framework for replying to *The Christian Education Journal's* invitation to give "a theologian's perspective on key issues for Christian educators." Systematics, as "theology in the round," takes up the major doctrines of historic Christianity—the *loci*. The loci are the locations, the places, the standard topics of Christian belief. Melanchthon in his *Loci Communes* put into usage the language of "common places" of theological attention. Systematic theology, therefore, is attention to the *commonplaces* of Christian teaching, relating them to one another and to a given time and place.

Today's outpouring of works in this genre ranges along a spectrum from "evangelical" through "ecumenical" to "experiential," according to the degree to which the context enters the processes of interpretation. Stated otherwise: works of systematics exist on a continuum determined by the degree to which either contemporary categories or historic formulations take precedence.

The commonplaces to which theologians return, ever and again, include anthropology, Christology, soteriology, ecclesiology, eschatology and "theology" (the doctrine of God), with their subsets (for example, under ecclesiology, sacramentology, missiology). Systematics also includes a discussion, usually at the beginning, of "how to" premises (variously described as methodology, epistemology, bibliology and so on).

Behind these technical terms—including the order in which they are treated—lie universal reference points in the faith of the church: the topics and sequence of the ecumenical creeds (Apostles' and Nicene); and basic to these, the biblical narrative from Genesis to Revelation, from creation to consummation. Perspectival disagreements abound, of course, on the content of each locus, depending on where one falls on the spectrum from retrieval to reconstruction. And, on occasion, a systematician will add a topic (for example, "Israelology" in a time of Jewish-Christian dialogue) or will argue for the alteration of the sequence. But in the main, the commonplaces are as described.

In this response, I take learnings from my discipline as it now seeks to retrieve, integrate and contextualize the commonplaces and to suggest their relationship to the work of Christian education in congregations.[8] The heart of my contention is: whatever else Christian educators do, and however they choose to do it, central to their vocation is the introduction of learners to the commonplaces of Christian belief. Fundamental to that task is clarity about the loci.

The Loci of Christian Education

"Narrative" is the perspective and organizing principle of this treatment of the commonplaces. A case can be made that the motif of narrative/story stays very close to Scripture itself with its "unfolding drama."[9] (This could account, in part, for the growing interest in the narrative motif among evangelical theologians.)[10] It has deep roots as well as in the ancient creeds, based as they are on the sequence of the three "missions" of the triune God—creation, reconciliation, sanctification—the divine "economy." While the warrants in Scripture and tradition are strong, narrative theology is clearly a contemporary movement, representing a response to the challenges of the present context and employing some of its idiom. Thus the commonplaces of church teaching will be treated as "chapters" in the Christian story, the *substance* of Christian education, in whatever setting it goes on, and by whatever method it is carried out. We take them up here in the usual sequence, minus the customary prolegomena on "authority and revelation."[11]

The Trinity

What distinguishes Christian belief in God from all other religious views is its teaching about the Trinity. Does this doctrine come front and center in Christian education today? If it does not, something basic to our identity gets short shrift. Further, an opportunity is missed to bring Christian faith to bear on critical contextual issues.

God is triune—three coeternal, coequal persons in one being. This ancient formula that seems so abstract to our pragmatic American minds is integral to the Christian story. It tells us that *what* God wills is grounded in *who* God is. God is a trinitarian Life Together, and wills that way for the world. The mutuality and equality in deity are not only the ground and goal of the unfolding biblical drama, but also the model for human relationships in both the church and society. The *diakonia* of the church in its mission to the world and the *koinonia* of the Christian community, rise out of the *kerygma* that proclaims the unity and partnership of the triune God.[12] So *didache* as introduction to the Trinity (and also *leitourgia* as the nourishment of trinitarian praise) can both interrelate the dimensions of the church's life and witness and contribute to the contextualizing of faith.

Creation

The opening chapter of the biblical Story grows out of the being and doing of the triune God. God calls the world into existence and invites it into relationship. Brought into being ex nihilo by its Maker, creation is a derivative and therefore not a divine good. It is to be honored and built up, but not worshiped. Here is a Christian foundation for an ecological ethic in a world awash in environmental peril, one that avoids the popular romanticizing of nature.

In this same chapter, human nature, made in the divine image, is granted special dignity and charged with special responsibility. What this singularity is and where its beginnings and endings are constitute the theological questions at the center of major cultural disputes from abortion to euthanasia. Fundamental issues of theological anthropology must, therefore, be on the agenda of today's Christian education.

A third dimension of creation, much on the minds of many

experimenting with cult and occult, is "supernature." There is theological work to do in church education programs in order to offer young and old an alternative to popular esoterica. In developing the biblical understanding of "powers and principalities" we can call upon our own rich tradition in response to fashions and fancies that run from New Age angelology to apocalyptic satanology.[13]

Fall

The Story tells of an invitation turned aside. In the imagery of the poet Weldon Johnson, the world shakes its fist in the face of its Maker. And so creation stumbles and falls.

Sin is not a welcome word in the ears of modernity, a fact the great psychiatrist Karl Menninger has documented in his *Whatever Became of Sin?*[14] But sin is part of the code language of Scripture, having to do with a fundamental chapter in the Story. Its misuse by Christians who trivialize it, or reduce it to the "when" and "where" questions of its origin and thus fail to speak about the "what" of original/universal sin, has contributed to its demise. But so have the naivetés of our Enlightenment past, and now the pretensions of a currently popular postmodernity.

The universal about-face from the divine beckoning has a profound impact on our personal and social histories. Reinhold Niebuhr reminded another generation that without the self-critical principle represented by the biblical doctrine of sin, movements for social change, as well as persons of moral and spiritual achievement, regularly fall prey to the arrogance of power. The corruptibility of our noblest efforts demonstrates the profundity of this biblical wisdom, as do the current self-righteous furies of both the religious right and the religious left.

The Fall has to do with nature and supernature as well as human nature. The issues of "theodicy" discussed in the adult study class reading Rabbi Kushner's *When Bad Things Happen to Good People* will find light shed on them from the classical Christian teaching that the whole creation does really "groan" in travail. In the Story, nature is well short of its new birth, the day when the wolf will dwell with the lamb. And "supernature" has its demonic as well as its angelic dimensions. This astringent realism about powers and principalities as well as persons can help that study group make their way in hope through their own pain and the larger troubles of our time.

Covenant

Sin has its consequences. But the times of Noah are remembered for the rainbow as well as the flood. The covenant with Noah is a critical chapter in the Story, sadly missing in too much of our pedagogy.

After the deluge, God promises to sustain the world through thick and thin. As the world is in the "holy keeping" of Providence, we are given enough light on the path ahead to keep the Tale going forward. In the Genesis accounts, the world's Sustainer grants glimpses of the good, the true, the beautiful and the holy to all creation, and gives it enough power with that light to make human life livable. The Noachic covenant has to do with "general revelation" and "common grace." While not the last Word, these are good words; while not the Great Light they are "little lights." Common grace/general revelation is the theological warrant for honoring and appropriating "secular" wisdom—from the use of the social sciences by Christian educators to the moral learnings we gain from the world's reformers. And it allows us as well to discern evidences of the holy in the world's religions.

Covenant in the unfolding drama is particular as well as universal. Two-thirds of Scripture have to do with the special covenant with Israel. Christian education deals with this inheritance from, and common ground with, Israel. And it must face into the twentieth century's Holocaust history. All this requires a hard struggle with the theological relationship of Christian faith to Judaism, including the knotty questions theologians call "supersessionism" and "antisupersessionism."[15] In this covenant chapter of the Story, God elects a people, brings them out of bondage into a land flowing with milk and honey, gives them a taste of *shalom,* the lost vision of the way the world should be, sets forth the decalogic laws of that new land—the love of God and neighbor—watches over Israel in its wandering ways, and with us makes Israel a partner in waiting for that day when the wolf will dwell with the lamb.

In the great saga of particular covenant, Israel proves to be as we all are, no lovers of the light of the Day-to-be. But God keeps the divine promises.

Jesus Christ

What can turn the world around? In our Story, it's not a "what" but a "Who." We take our name from him. Jesus Christ—*one of us,* born of woman, sharing our common lot, dying at our hands—yet One *more than us,* conceived by the Spirit, exorcising evil, forgiving sin, rising from the dead. As the ancient doctrine of Incarnation has it: truly human, truly God, truly one.

Our forebears' theological language for the "person of Christ" attempts to situate the New Testament accounts of Jesus within the drama we are tracing that began in the intratrinitarian Life. Indeed, as John expresses it:

> In the beginning was the Word, and the Word was with God, and the Word was God. . . . And the Word became flesh and lived among us. (John 1:1, 14)

The eternal Word, the divine Self-communication of Life Together, came among us in Jesus Christ, the divine-human who alone can turn the tale around.

There *is* a What to this Who, traditionally called "the work of Christ." It has to do with contesting the powers of sin, evil and death that from the beginning have stood athwart the divine purposes. The Story tells us that in Galilee, at Calvary and on Easter morning, these powers have met their match. Hence the simplest profession of Christian faith made by the church member: "I accept Jesus Christ as Lord and Savior."

Our Reformation ancestors described Christ's redemptive ministry (the doctrine of the Atonement) in terms of a "threefold office": prophetic, priestly and royal. This symbol continues as a timely teaching device for it brings together the varied emphases of current partisans, avoiding their reductionist tendencies: the witness of the "liberals" who accent Christ's Galilean work as example and teacher (the prophetic office), the witness of the "conservatives" who stress Christ's salvation from sin on Calvary's cross (the priestly office), and the witness of the political theologies and Eastern Christians who in very different ways point to the grounds for hope in the Easter Liberator/Victor (the royal office).

In Christian education, whether articulated or not, assumptions about both the person and work of Christ are *inescapable.* Unexamined assumptions leave practitioners at the mercy of either the culture's agenda or the loudest voices in our corner of the church. And they leave learners impoverished, denied the riches of the classical tradition. Incarnation and Atonement are at the heart of church learning.

The Church

Continuing our narrative reading of Christian doctrine, the resurrection and ascension of Jesus Christ are followed by the Pentecostal birth of the church. In Luke-Acts's powerful imagery, the ascent of Christ makes possible the descent of the Spirit—the risen Son/Sun of God sending down "tongues of fire." Thus the Light of a new Day brings with it the power to make the turn away from Night, to "see the light"—to see *in* the light the brother and sister in Christ, and see *by* the light the neighbor in need. Seeing the light—the *metanoia* we call conversion; seeing in the light the brother and sister—the *koinonia* of the Christian community; seeing by the light—the *diakonia* of Samaritan care—all are on the agenda of the Christian educator.

Standard ecclesiology declares the church to be the body of Christ, a divine-human organism with the Spirit as its animating breath and Christ as its Head. This body is washed by the waters of baptism and fed at its holy table. And the Spirit brings the Word from God's mouth in season and out. Sacraments/ordinances are a major teaching task in today's church.

Ministries are given to the body by Christ to sustain its life. Some are custodians of its identity, nurturing it in the memory of who— and whose—it is. Others are stewards of its vitality, enabling it to walk and work in the world. Christian education is a key part of the ministries and mission of the church. Its roots are in the ancient teaching office. Its call is to nurture the body of Christ. With the pastor, the teacher is commissioned to "equip the saints for the work of ministry, for building up the body of Christ" (Eph 4:12).

Salvation

We spoke about the church as those "seeing the light." "Subjective soteriology," so understood, is inextricable from ecclesiology. But salvation is a broader subject in its own right, its range neither identical to nor circumscribed by the church.

In the Story, salvation is from personal sin and guilt before God. The evangelical gift to the church at large is its witness to this central Christian conviction.

> Therefore since we are justified by faith, we have peace with God
> through our Lord Jesus Christ. (Rom 5:1)

How and when the Christian educator makes a contribution to this call to personal faith is an open question. That the church's teachers have a role in this ministry is indisputable. Even those not of evangelical persuasion do not hesitate to relate their work to "sanctification," the partner to "justification." Vocational self-understanding cannot afford to ignore the minutes of the last meeting on all these matters—the classical theological debates and distinctions in subjective soteriology concerning justification and sanctification.

Salvation in Scripture, according to the venerable Cruden's *Concordance,* is from "trouble or danger" as well as from "sin and its consequences." Here Christian education faces its constituency toward today's troubles and dangers: oppression, war, poverty, hunger, crime, sickness, sorrow, loneliness, ignorance . . . all the social, economic, political and personal maladies of our time. Salvation is liberation from these evils as well as freedom from sin and guilt before God. As Karl Barth vividly put it, we do our teaching and preaching with the Bible in one hand and the daily newspaper in the other. In soteriology as in all the other doctrines, the text and the context are inseparable.

Consummation

Salvation, in Christian teaching, has a not-yet as well as a now dimension. Soteriology in the future tense is "eschatology," the doctrine of last things. Narratively considered, it is the last chapter of the biblical Story, the consummation of the purposes of God.

With a modesty appropriate to the subject, the central tradition of Christian theology has spoken about the End in the language of metaphor, not metaphysics. As we see "through a glass darkly"—not through a picture window, clearly—the creedal affirmations have the character of stained glass. They portray in vivid color "the resurrection of the dead," "the return of Christ," "the final judgment," "the everlasting life." As such, they let in enough light to read our hymnbooks and sing praises to the God who will finally vindicate the suffering Savior, right every wrong, and be all and in all. Eschatology, so understood, is Christian theodicy, the confidence in God's Future that knows of nothing that *"will* be able to separate us from the love of God in Christ Jesus our Lord" (Rom 8:39).

Consummation has to do with the penultimate as well as the ultimate Future, life after death before the last things. While mystery is appropriate in these next-to-last things as well, the same sure hope is heard, an eternal life with God which death cannot sever.

If these doctrinal basics about both our imminent and ultimate futures were the regular substance of Christian education, our parishioners would have nourishment of such solidity that the spiritual and apocalyptic junk foods of the day would lose their allure.

Conclusion

The contribution a systematic theologian can make to the current conversation in Christian education has more to do with the importance and character of theology *in* the discipline than the theology *of* it. Hence the attention here to the commonplaces of Christian teaching. In our respective ministries, we are stewards of these mysteries. May that partnership work toward a faithful telling of the Story in our time.

4

Centralities in the Seminaries[†]

ARE SEMINARY TEACHERS CHURCHLESS AGNOSTICS? PURVEYORS OF THE culture's latest fads and fancies? One more evidence of the decadence of mainline churches? Some recent media reports on the molders of student minds paint this picture.

Stacked up on my desk are 115 sets of syllabi of basic courses in theology from schools around the country that tell a very different story. They are part of information gathered from colleagues in systematics who shared what they are doing in formative, required and often year-long courses, and where they believe we are going in theology today. I wrote to all I could find in North America from memberships of theological societies and catalog listings—219—and received 140 replies, representing 92 institutions. Respondents are a cross-section of teachers of systematic theology, mostly from denominational seminaries (Protestant and Roman Catholic), university

[†]This essay was based on my 1991 presidential address to the American Theological Society, published as "Reorientation and Retrieval in Systematic Theology," *The Christian Century* 108 (June 26-July 3, 1991): 653-56.

divinity schools, and evangelical seminaries.

What colleagues do or think is the case, of course, is not the same as what *should* be so. The present mood could be quite wrong. As Bonhoeffer put it, we should not be "servile before fact." However, knowing the actual lay of the land in this case challenges many of the current caricatures of the church and its institutions. And further, the Christian community, and in this case some of its "doctors," is an important resource (not *the source*) for interpreting the faith in our time and place. What follows is a glimpse of life in our classrooms, with a comment here and there from one teacher.

Diversity

The first discovery is that sweeping generalizations about what doctrinal positions are "in" or "out" make little sense. *Many* theologies are among us. This diversity is different from other epochs; for example, the time when a Princeton scholasticism dominated large parts of the nineteenth-century Protestant seminary landscape, or even the recent period when the books of "neo-orthodoxy" were at the least the common reference point for theological debate.

Diversity itself comes in a variety of shapes and sizes:

1. *Contextual perspectives* are high profile. The dramatic emergence of African-American, feminist, womanist, North American Hispanic, Third World/Two Thirds World, laity, Native American, Asian, Asian-American peoples and points of view is a fact of life in much of the field of systematics; it is minimal but growing in the teaching corps of systematicians, significantly present in required readings and in supplemental bibliography, and also through guest lecturers.

And now the presence in seminary of large numbers of second-career students, including those who bring histories of personal and vocational crises, together with an increasingly multicultural constituency, bring its own kind of contextuality. Thus theological reality-testing from the workplace, family life, cultural ferment, and contexts of oppression goes on through the agency of students themselves.

2. *Schools of thought* take us from contextuality to overarching theological frameworks. Some respondents felt that this breaks down

into two basic categories today: the "postliberal" and the "revisionist" positions, or the "Yale" and "Chicago" schools, or just the Lindbeckians and the Tracyites. A few concluded: "What else is new? It's Barth and Tillich all over again, the old kerygmatic and apologetic options."

The oversimplification of this division, however, is soon apparent when evangelical theology makes its appearance. Even within this major alternative, a case could be made for at least six subsets: "old evangelicals," "new evangelicals," "justice and peace evangelicals," "charismatic evangelicals," "fundamentalists," and "ecumenical evangelicals." Add to that the variety of liberation theologies plus the transcendental Thomist, the neo-Calvinist, the confessional Lutheran, the Anglo-Catholic, the process, pluralist, the unrepentant neo-orthodox and neoliberal, the Eastern Orthodox, the three kinds of narrative theology and more. We may need a moratorium on typologizing schools of thought until the air clears.

3. A case can be made for an easily overlooked third kind of diversity, *movements.* These are points of view and perspectives that have a significant *institutional* base and momentum. With as many students in the fifteen schools represented as all the rest put together, along with parachurch networks, mass media outlets and so forth, evangelicalism is a major new player on the theological scene. And there are other points of view with similar social dynamisms. African-American theologies have a black church and seminary base and North American Hispanic theologies may be developing along parallel lines, as well as feminist theologies with their support structures.

Two other movements discernible, but with lower profiles, are the long-standing ecumenical movement with special momentum these days in bilateral dialogues and interfaith forums, and the charismatic/Pentecostal movement now producing its own systematic works and nurturing large constituencies in its schools and churches.

4. Often missed in the map-making of theology today, but now increasingly asserting itself, is the presence of *ecclesial traditions.* Being a Lutheran, Roman Catholic, Reformed, Baptist, Eastern Orthodox . . . figures increasingly in the picture of theological pluralism, and in the very specific area of systematics curricula. It emerges in

the required reading to be discussed and the stress on church roots in both school and faculty comments.

What we do with all these differences is, of course, the question. If one believes in a Corinthian catholicity (1 Cor 12, 13)—the potential for mutual *enrichment* by diversity, as Paul contended in the face of the partisanships in the church at Corinth—then this is a moment of special opportunity. It requires, however, the acknowledgment of limitations, the recognition of the *partiality* of perspective, and a commensurate openness to learning from others. If we do not seize upon the promise of this moment through what we might call "the mutual conversation, consolation and correction of the brothers and sisters" (to borrow and edit a phrase of Luther's), we could be in for a period of theological balkanization . . . or Beirutization—armed camps firing away at each other from their places of epistemological privilege.

Retrieval
Diversity, yes. But all across the spectrum, some commonalities are discernible. The first and most visible is the motif of "retrieval." That is, our teachers of doctrine/constructive theology say, and show by their syllabi, that we are and should be about the business of recovering the *theological heritage*. The period of cafeteria theology, "adhocracy," preoccupation with prolegomena or unremitting contemporaneity, seems to be over. Know the tradition!

The reasons for retrieval vary.

1. Many assert the heritage because they believe it to be true as is, and hold that it has been lost in a recent era of theological adventurism. This view is to be found in a pronounced way in evangelical seminaries, and to a significant extent in mainline schools as well. Its espousal is *not* to be equated with the outright rejection of advocacy perspectives nor with the denial of the importance of contextual and cultural encounter, for these things are regularly linked to retrieval. But the stress is clearly laid much more on recovery than on "relevance."

2. Others also believe in retrieving the heritage but are more concerned to keep contextuality in tandem with it. However, they too worry about the erosion of theological identity and want to bring

"the message" to parity, and more, with "the situation." While tradition must always be reread in terms of the context, these people assert that this can only be done if the past formulations are at least known. Teachers who want to recontextualize are often stunned by how little familiarity there is with that heritage in their students and in the churches. So the bringing to higher visibility of the tradition becomes a priority, even as contextuality and contemporaneity are also stressed.

3. A few give attention to the tradition because they want a foil for the radical reformulation they believe is demanded by qualitatively different times. They hold that the inherited theology has either been hostage to an oppressor class, race or sex, or works out of a dying paradigm now being replaced by new sensitivities to world religions, cosmic consciousness, historicist realities, postmodern ambiguities and so on. But these innovators contend that we also need to know what *has been* the case in order to sharpen awareness of our new age and to appreciate the power of necessarily new proposals.

How the tradition is recovered varies in all three of these accents on retrieval. But there is one feature that appears in most basic courses in systematics: the covering of the traditional loci by use of one or more texts that touch on each major doctrine. The spread of texts is very interesting.

Current texts that cover all the doctrines predominate. In mainline seminaries, often more than one such text is required, reflecting to some extent the desire to give students an alternate reading of basic Christian convictions. Or, in all kinds of seminaries, one or more texts will be supplemented with required or suggested selections from other points of view on specific doctrines along with assigned readings in collections of historical excerpts.

The most dramatic development in this area of current systematics works is the number of them that have been written in the past twenty years. Over seventy new projects in full-scale systematic theology or "introductions" have been launched, ranging in length from one to seven volumes. And other major projects are under way. The writing of systematic theologies—perhaps also the production of many new dictionaries, encyclopedias and biblical commentaries—is a significant sign of efforts at both retrieval and "getting it all together."

Another kind of resource for covering the traditional loci is the use of "the giants" and near-giants of the twentieth century. Here the works of Karl Barth stand out above others. But the writings of Rahner and Tillich also appear, and the old standby John Macquarrie, who was writing systematics when virtually no one else was, is still used in a few places.

Some teachers settle only for "classical texts," or do so in conjunction with resources of the two previous types. Calvin is widely read, but so are Luther, Aquinas, Augustine, Schleiermacher, Wesley, and a scattering of the early Fathers and medieval Mothers. Excerpts from these authors are also assigned as sections of volumes of readings, along with dictionary entries. And in conjunction with, or without, historic interpreters, there often appear confessional, catechetical and creedal texts. Again, "know who you are"—your tradition—is an increasingly strong note sounded.

While classic and contemporary texts are the major resources for covering doctrines, a few schools avoid all use of formal systematics works and rely instead on selections from, or full volumes of, a variety of authors, often with different perspectives on given topics.

Whatever else this variegated pattern of retrieval means, a few modest generalizations seem apt: (1) The charge that seminary teachers are now "post-Christian" is a misrepresentation of the first order. At the very least, the recovery of the tradition puts students in touch with the assumptions that function in the hymnbooks and prayer books of their prospective parishioners, the lections from which they will preach and the ordination papers they must write. And much more. (2) Retrieval is not, as such, repristination. The character of many, if not most, of the readings and virtually all of the respondents' comments, indicate a desire to interpret the tradition in the light of today's issues. That is our next point.

Contemporaneity

Contemporaneity is a broad term for making connections with time and place. No galvanizing center of contemporary concern is discernible in North American systematicians today—as may be the case, for example, in the seminary world of East or West Germany or South Africa, with collapsing and challenged ideologies, or in Latin Amer-

ica with socioeconomic perils and proposals to the fore. Nevertheless, very high on the agenda in our setting is the plight of the
marginalized. We have already spoken of this under the rubric of
diversity, as the victims and the voiceless rising to demand a hearing.
But here we note a much wider concern to confront the oppression
of women, the rights of African-Americans and Hispanics, the agony
of the homeless and hungry, the battering of women, the abuse of
children, the tragedy of AIDS, the Holocaust history of the Jewish
people, the decimation of the Amerindian. The hermeneutics of
suspicion seem to have hit home, in the sense of a growing awareness
that one can't recover the fullness of the tradition itself without the
expansion of vision beyond the captivities to one or another wielder
of social power.

"Contemporaneity" also includes a range of other cultural concerns. Sometimes they are summed up under the rubric of "globali-
zation"—North American systematicians becoming aware of
pandemic hunger, disease and war, and of the different concerns and
perceptions of reality found around the world—religious and otherwise. Developments in science, especially the implications of the
new physics, uncharted medical and biomedical questions, are also
given attention, albeit only here and there. Theologies of creation
are in evidence, showing the effects of both the environmental crisis
and new cosmic horizons. In Roman Catholic seminaries philosophy,
contemporary and classical, is given more attention than in other
places, usually in "fundamental theology" courses conjoined to systematics ones. The increased awareness of contemporary religious
pluralism is everywhere to be found, with curricular attention and
theological response reflecting the full range of diversity earlier
indicated.

Church Commitment

By specific assertion and by its presence in course content, "the
church" is the environment in which theology is and ought to be
done. Here the evidence in the teaching of systematics is on collision
course with journalistic and even academic generalizations. Consider the refrain expressed variously by these "testimonies," all from
mainline seminary faculty:

Whatever else dogmatic/systematic theology . . . might be for, it has to be for proclamation. Theology has to be done so as literally to drive its practitioners from the lectern to the pulpit.

I am interested in how the believing, worshiping, praying community of Jesus Christ *appropriates* and then lives the Bible and its Tradition. . . . Systematic theology must begin in prayer (communal and individual), be sustained by it, and even end there because God is always the ever-great Mystery.

I am committed unashamedly to teaching Christian doctrine and draw a clear distinction between that which is taught in a secular environment . . . and what is confessionally committed (what should, I believe, be taught to prospective ministers in Christ's church).

Theology finds its primary task in assisting the community (of faith) to listen, worship, preach and serve.

My lectures tend to emphasize a *lex orandi* standpoint—doctrines informed by and grounded in the church at worship, and prayer.

And from a syllabus:

On most weeks, one hour of the Thursday class will be devoted to dealing with *theological issues* involved in pastoral situations. . . . For each pastoral situation, the student . . . is expected to isolate the theological issue or issues involved; explain where s/he would go/have gone for resources to deal with that issue.

And from an exam:

Set forth the doctrine of the Person of Christ implicit or explicit in the Christmas hymn by Charles Wesley, "Hark the Herald Angels Sing," and evaluate it from your perspective.

And more of the same in many places, but of course not everywhere. Perhaps the *parish* critics who bewail the "abstractions" of theological teachers will be as surprised to know of these churchly concerns in systematics classes as the *Atlantic* reader of Paul Wilkes's "The Hands That Would Shape Our Souls" (December 1990). Contrary to the latter's skepticism about today's seminaries, the hands of many theology teachers do hold hymnals.

Whither?

For this teacher, the accents on retrieval, contemporaneity and church commitment are genuine signs of hope. So too for a hundred or so pastors who responded to a parallel inquiry I made on the state of theology to check how those on the front line of teaching felt about the same things. They spoke much about the "disarray," "confusion" and "decline" of theology in congregations and urged upon seminary teachers attention to the "foundations" with clear linkage to current issues and the mission of the church.

Yet a question mark lingers. What happens in theology may, humanly speaking, finally hinge on what we do with the fourth phenomenon, diversity. If we resist the temptation to tribalism—the claim that our restricted angle of vision has a God's-eye view of the truth—then there is the possibility of a mutually enriching conversation, one that could eventuate in a more ecumenical understanding of Christian faith, an "evangelical catholicity" as the old Mercersburg theologians called it. Or, to edit a bit the memorable phrases of Rupert Meldinius:

In perspectives, diversity
In essentials, catholicity
In all things, charity.

5

I Believe in
the Resurrection
of the Body[†]

REINHOLD NIEBUHR TELLS OF LONG DISCUSSIONS AMONG SEMINARY SENIORS
in his class on the closing phrases of the Apostles' Creed. Preparing
for their ordination exams, they agonized over whether moderns
could confess *this* part of the ancient faith. The resurrection of the
body?

Twenty years later, however, Niebuhr could declare:

Some of us have been persuaded to take the stone which we then
rejected and to make it the head of the corner. . . . There is no part
of the Apostolic Creed which . . . expresses the whole genius of
the Christian faith more neatly than just that despised phrase, "I
believe in the resurrection of the body."[1]

Yet modernity has nine lives. What seemed to have been transcended
by Niebuhrian neo-orthodoxy is still much among us a half century
later. For many of our contemporaries, tombs still do not get emptied—not Christ's, not ours.

What then do we do with the second Advent lections? The Easter

---

[†]This essay was first published in *Interpretation* 46 (January 1992): 42-52.

texts? The parishioner's furrowed brow at graveside?

Niebuhr would be pleased to know that "postmodernism" has forced some reconsideration of Enlightenment assumptions about what can and cannot happen to the dead. Here and there, prominent theologians are ready to declare once again, "I believe in the resurrection of the body and the life everlasting"! And more: "He shall come again to judge the living and the dead." The confidence in reason's ability to know all, and thus to disqualify ancient doctrine, is now seen to be itself a piece of dogma, one with a checkered history.[2] Demythologizers of modernity have encouraged us to relearn our own language and tell our own story. And retrieval of the tradition includes the tale of Things to Come.

Yes, let us recover our own version of how the world works, and see again our forebears' visions of the End. But not only because postmodern critics have now decreed it safe to do so! Taking our cues from the culture's self-criticism could be yet one more Babylonian captivity. Especially so when the perspectivism that often accompanies the critique of modernity is reluctant to make truth claims about our "language game."[3] Eschatological rejuvenation, with all the mystery that rightly attends it, has to do with an "assurance of things hoped for" (Heb 11:1). The "resurrection of the body" is assertable as ontologically so, as well as confessionally proper.

The regaining of our eschatological sight is also necessary for making our way past today's various tempting bypaths. Without it, there is much stumbling toward the New Ageisms and millennialisms of the hour.[4] With cultic esoterica and end-time eschatology dominating the airwaves and shopping mall bookstores shelves, the modest assertions of the creed are treasures waiting to be rediscovered. Classical eschatology has now become a countercultural option.

Christ's Resurrection and Ours

Christian talk about things to come begins with the One who has *already* arrived. Assertions about the future are grounded in decisive past events in the history of Jesus Christ. On this point, secular futurology and biblical eschatology are of the same mind. Both base their projections on discernible trajectories from within history. The secular futurologist speaks of a "thirteen multifold trend" traceable to the late Middle Ages—urbanization, literacy, population growth, scientific inquiry, and so on.[5] Christian faith points to the past's singular Easter happenings. Both the futurist and the believer know the difference between hope and fantasy, the former being rooted in anticipatory signs and the latter devoid of such credentials. "The third day he rose again from the dead. . . . I believe in the resurrection of the body."

Embodiment

As with the risen Jesus, so with us, the consummation of the divine purpose is a full-blooded end. Jesus' resurrection was no ectoplasmic appearance or oblong blur. The New Testament accounts are of encounter with an embodied Christ. "Reach out your hand and put it in my side" (Jn 20:27). The bold physicality makes us wince. "My Lord and my God!" (Jn 20:28). For Christians, tangibility is a portent of ultimate things to come: no vaporous soul aloft forever in spiritual skies, no passage of a droplet self into an eternal sea, no everlasting memory in the mind of God, nor wistful solace based on our influence on generations to come.[6] Rather, "God gives it a body" (1 Cor 15:38).

But, but . . . Yes, Paul had the same "buts." He tells us that there are bodies, and then there are bodies. "There are both heavenly bodies and earthly bodies. . . . So it is with the resurrection of the dead" (1 Cor 15:40, 42). Indeed, the paradox takes us once again to the "first fruits" of final hope. The accounts of the risen Jesus are strange indeed. A body that dines but "vanishes" (Lk 24:30-31). One that can be touched (Jn 20:27), but not "held on to" (Jn 20:17). What else but a preview of the mystery of our own resurrection: "If there is a physical body there is also a spiritual body. . . . This perishable body puts on imperishability" (1 Cor 15:44, 54). We know how to say what it isn't: not mortal "flesh and blood" (1 Cor 15:50), not the same as the seed sown, not the perishable. "Apophatic"—negative—eschatology!

Paul's reserve, as well as his both/and dialectic, anticipates the resistance to either/or oversimplifications that will mark doctrinal disputes for millennia to come. Partisans fix upon either the human or divine, the physical or the "spiritual," from the christological controversies to the sacramental debates. And in each case, mystery must be honored; the Pauline paradox must assert itself.[7]

While it is hard to say just what the eschatological "both/and" means, we end with the apostolic finger pointing to Jesus. He rose again, fully but differently, "the firstborn from among the dead" (Col 1:18). And so shall we. "Thanks be to God who has given us the victory through our Lord Jesus Christ" (1 Cor 15:57).

Universality

Victory, yes, for "those who belong to Christ" (1 Cor 15:23). How about all the others? Classical teaching is fairly uniform here. *All* the dead are raised: "There will be a resurrection of both the righteous and the unrighteous" (Acts 24:15). But some, even a few prominent evangelicals of late, have tempered the wind to the shorn sheep with the defense of "annihilationism."[8] They hold that the destiny of the unworthy is dissolution; resurrection/immortality is conditional. The motive here may be the challenge of theories of ultimate judgment beholden to punitive cultural practices. But there are better ways of questioning retributive eschatologies then abandoning the clear biblical refrains of accountability. (We shall presently examine an alternative.) The resurrection of the dead is both a final hope and a final reckoning.

Eschatology and Ethics

The deeper one moves into the classical themes of resurrection, the more restless even our postmodern minds become: "What does all this have to do with the perils of nuclear war, the spread of AIDS, justice for the poor, crime in the streets and the rights of battered women? In the end, is not the focus on the not yet one more escape avenue from the now?"

Anything but, according to one of the great ethicists of our time. James Luther Adams points out that commitment to social change is correlated with the kind of images that mark our eschatology. If we envisage our final destiny as that of an immortal soul, an ahistorical piety and morality invariably follow. If Last Things are portrayed as the destiny of isolated persons, an individualistic ethic is predictable. In contrast, the resurrection of the *body* carries with it the mandate to care here and now for the hungry, homeless and abused. And the understanding of the End as a new order—the kingdom of God, the New Jerusalem—means that God wills here as well as hereafter a just and peaceful society and habitable cities. Further, the anticipation of a new heaven and new earth (Rev 21:1), the ultimate redemption of nature—"the river of the water of life" (Rev 22:1) and "the tree of life" with its twelve kinds of fruits (Rev 22:22)—is a relentless ecological imperative. Eschatological visions, embodied hopes—micro, meso and macro—have radical ethical implications.

Jürgen Moltmann has constructed his theology around just these refrains.[9] What we dream forms what we do. Hence the importance of eschatological recovery for social change. The *confidence* that the End will truly consummate the purposes of God, as anticipated by exodus and Easter, energizes the believing community to set up signs on the way to that kingdom and city. Hope mobilizes while despair paralyzes. The *content* of that End—glorified bodies, the holy city with its jewel-like radiance (Rev 21:10), crystal waters and flourishing forests—renders unacceptable emaciated bodies, cities of the homeless and hapless, poisonous rivers and decimated forests. Eschatology makes us pilgrims and strangers in the wilderness short of New Creation, and disturbers of the facile peace of the way things are.

Other Eschatological Windows

Already we have introduced linkages between the resurrection of the body and allied visions of the End—a renewed history and cosmos. The classical creeds identify four interlocking themes. Joining the resurrection of the body/the dead are "the return of Christ," "final judgment" and "everlasting life."[10] The ecumenical consensus on these four affirmations is a good guide to the future, helping us avoid the parched deserts of eschatological agnosticism or the entangling jungles of apocalyptic speculation. These refrains tell us more than a skeptical modernity will allow but less than zealous premillennialists demand.

Like the assertion of the resurrection of the body, the associated affirmations make distinct truth claims. Yet each also honors the mystery and observes the constraints of biblical modesty. They are, so to speak, stained-glass windows of the Future. Translucent but not transparent, their rich imagery hints at what will be. We "see through a glass darkly," not through a picture window clearly. And we get just enough light to read our hymnals and sing praises to the One who comes—rather than read intricate timetables of arrival. Eschatology is doxology.

The Return of Christ

"He will come again" declares the creed, echoing the numerous second advent references (Mt 24:30; 26:24; Lk 21:27, Acts 1:11; 3:20-21; 1 Cor 4:5; 15:23; 2 Cor 1:14; Phil 1:6; 2:16; 3:20, etc.). We have seen that picture in the chancel. The text and the tradition are telling us that the death of Jesus Christ is not the final destiny of their Lord. The ear of faith has heard Easter apostolic testimony, and the eye of faith sees this now, even in a dim light. But the ear of all and the eye of all will also discover it to be so at the End.

The return of Christ validates publicly the resurrection of Christ. And the embodiment theme continues here, for the One who comes again is the incarnate Lord. Thus our Advent season preaching (which is trifocal, the lections covering messianic expectation, the preparation for Christmas and the *parousia*) fixes on a multidimensional hope: hope for our historical future, body and soul, illumined by the sure and certain hope of Christ's return, a sun risen from the resurrection dawn.[11]

But can you hear the murmurings about all these biblical metaphors of the end time? All around us are folk who will not settle for mystery and modesty. They want to hear more about the when, the where and the how of the return. And there are advertisers of apocalptyic quite ready to provide maps, timetables and blueprints of the not yet.[12]

Some of the appeal of "pre-trib pre-mil" dispensationalism and its kin has to do with our own failures in mainline churches to address the eschatological questions here explored. Often we throw up a wall instead of opening a window. But, finally, we cannot give the curious what they want—clear and distinct photos of what is to be. Not if we follow our own charter:

It is not for you to know the times or periods that the Father has
set by his own authority. (Acts 1:7)
There are more things to be said on this, and we shall return to the
issue in "Pastoral Questions." But for now, we attend to the word:
"About that day and hour no one knows" (Mt 24:36).

Final Judgment

"He will come again to judge the living and the dead." Christ returns
for a purpose. The vindication of his life, teaching, death and
resurrection entails our facing up to the response we make to the gift
given. And who can stand at this latter day when our sins of
commission and omission are disclosed in all their starkness by the
divine light? Only a graced faith saves, here or hereafter.

The Great Assize raises many issues, most of which take us well
beyond our resurrection theme. But the eschatological windows are
in the same building, so we make mention of one question: *who*
shares with Christ final glorification as well as resurrection?

Does the judgment of Christ end with the rigor of "double destination," or the embrace of "universalism"? The majority opinion over
the centuries, with an arsenal of texts, opts for the former. God will
"separate people one from another as a shepherd separates the sheep
from the goats" (Mt 25:32-33 so also Lk 16:19-31; Jn 3:36; 5:25-29; 2
Thess 1:9; Heb 6:8; 9:27; Rev 14:10-11). And an ultra-Calvinism adds
its accent: "double *pre*destination."

A minority view chooses the second way, with fewer biblical
warrants but a conviction that Timothy 2:4 is the key: "God our Savior
. . . desires everyone to be saved and to come to the knowledge of
the truth." God does what God wills, it is said, hence a universal
homecoming.

All doctrine bears the marks of its setting. And sometimes the
context takes charge of the text. Do we have that here? In the first
case, we have an eschatology based on a retributive penology that
exacts in kind, or more, from the criminal. In the second case, we
have a benign future beholden to Enlightenment confidences that
either God is too kind to hold us accountable or we are too good to
be so judged.

Can the accents of each be held together in eschatology (as in

Christology) by asserting *both* the tough and the tender love of Christ? Yes, there is accountability, judgment and punishment as befits the holiness of God. Yes, there is the compassion, acceptance and vulnerability that marks the love of God. To assert both is to consider that the coals of divine love are lasting, but not *ever*lasting. Love chastens with rehabilitation in view. But finally, the doctrinal paradox can only be explored, not explained. We cannot declare that God *will* save everyone, as the universalist does who claims to know too much about the final will and way of God. The homecoming of all is an article of *hope*, not an article of faith.[13]

Everlasting Life

"I believe in the . . . resurrection of the body and the life everlasting." Our last theme is the neighboring window, "life everlasting." And it is ablaze with many scenes—personal, social, cosmic.

In one corner is Revelation's own image:

Then I saw between the throne and the four living creatures and among the elders a Lamb standing as if it had been slaughtered. (Rev 5:6)

What a sight! Everlasting life means that "the pure in heart . . . will see God" (Mt 5:8). In one long tradition of the church, the fulfillment of personal communion is "the vision of God."

So in the rich images and language of the End, the *visio Dei* is a way of expressing the personal dimension of the last things.

But there is more. As noted earlier, biblical eschatology is corporate as well as individual, the commonwealth of God as well as the beatific vision.

The nations will walk by its light, and the kings of the earth will bring their glory into it. (Rev 21:24)

Thus human beings will see *by* the light as well as "see the light," discerning the path to "glory" and walking together on it. The goal is the kingdom that lies ahead with the city of God at its center. And yet more, for the final liberation and reconciliation of all things includes the healing of nature as well as self and society. The creation no longer groans but rejoices:

Then I heard every creature in heaven and on earth, and under the earth and in the sea, and all that is in them, singing, "To the

one seated on the throne and to the Lamb be blessing and honor
and glory and might forever and ever!" (Rev 5:13)
Our window makes a place for the wolf and the lamb, the leopard
and the kid lying down together. And all around them

the mountains and the hills . . . burst into song, and all the trees
. . . clap their hands. (Is 55:12)

The panorama portrayed near the end of the book of Revelation is
the model for the full window of Christian eschatology. We use it
almost always at burial, for in the face of death it says what we believe
about all the dimensions of everlasting life.

See, the home of God is among mortals.
He will dwell with them;
they will be his peoples,
and God himself will be with them;
he will wipe every tear from their eyes.
Death will be no more;
mourning and crying and pain will be no more,
for the first things have passed away. (Rev 21:3-4)

Pastoral Questions

Though we have examined the broad outlines of classical teaching
on the resurrection of the body and related themes, the pastor will
be confronted with puzzles that are not always addressed in these
great affirmations of the Ultimate Future. We conclude with a few of
the quandaries parishioners often face, and to which response can
be made by inference from the ancient framework.

1. *After the funeral service, a participant says:* "The Scripture meant
a lot to me. So did your words of consolation. But where is ____ now?"

Consider some of the replies to be heard, by the pastor, and also
by others, here and there:

☐ "His soul is with God while his body is in the ground."

☐ "Her soul is with God, her body is in the ground, but the two will
be united at the resurrection."

☐ "He died right into the world to come and therefore now has a
resurrected body, because there is no time in eternity."

☐ "We do not know or need to know the particulars, but only that
all will be well."

☐ "Well, we just don't know."

☐ "She is making a long journey, transmigrating we hope to a higher plane or a better next life in this world."

☐ "I don't know, but there's this medium on route 88 that may be able to put you in touch with him."

All these are hopeful answers, of course. We do not mention the more dyspeptic, sometimes thought but not often said. Does our framework allow for some modest inferences that address this poignant question?

While the weight of Scripture and tradition is placed on the ultimate not yet and its four emphases, there are indicators about the penultimate future. For one, time does seem to be honored, as is appropriate to a historical religion, with no clear warrant of a foreshortened resurrection that dissociates our fulfillment from that of a transfigured world. Hence, the long tradition of an "intermediate state" in which what we are then is not yet what we shall be. For another, while the interim state is described by some as "soul sleep," much of the church has taken the "awake" texts as decisive (Lk 16:19-31; 23:43; Rev 6:9), giving them a strong turn in eucharistic theology by association with the "communion of saints." Thus we are invited in the sacrament to join them even now around the throne in their songs of praise to God. Combined with this may be elaborate theories of mutual interaction between the dead and the living. But increasingly, these claims are muted or missing with the stress put (as in the Mercersburg theology) on praying *with* the saints.

Tradition is corrigible, of course, and the association of it with neo-Platonic construals of the intermediate state—the soul as a spiritual substance detached from the body[14]—is now widely challenged.[15] But if the resurrection of the body is the ultimate destiny, what then do we have to say to the parishioner's question about the penultimate journey? If "soul" were understood not as a detached ethereality but as the unique self-in-relationship-to-God (as in 1 Jn 3:2), then it surely does continue after death. If we can let go the hypercuriosity about "how" that takes place and be content with the strong "that" of Scripture, we will save ourselves from much fruitless and unbiblical speculation. In the end, we do just this *liturgically* in the recitation of the memorable cadences of Romans 8 at every burial, ones that conclude with the resounding assurance that nothing "will be able to separate us from the love of God in Christ Jesus our Lord" (Rom 8:39). An eternal life that begins in this world, by grace through faith, will not be severed at death.

2. *In the adult church school class, a raised hand:* "I heard a minister say on TV yesterday a lot more about the end times than we ever hear in church. He told us about 'the rapture,' the seven years of tribulation, the battle of Armageddon, the thousand years of peace and plenty, things happening right now in the Middle East . . . Just what is all that?"

Well, we'd better have some answers. There is a "theology of hope" of sorts in apocalypticism, one that draws multitudes in times of peril and places of hopelessness. And there are passages of Scripture with apocalyptic intent. Response to our inquirer requires clarity of hermeneutic.

Presupposed in our dealings with eschatology so far has been the centrality of *theological* and *ecclesial* modes of interpretation. That is, a text is understood in the light of canonical refrains read christologically ("theological" exegesis), and with the help of consensus points in the long Christian tradition ("ecclesial" exegesis). We invite our inquirer to look at the creeds we say and the hymns we sing. They have to do with the great thats and whats of the future, not its when, where and hows. So we are not going to trade on the fears and frenzies of the hour with maps of the kingdom to come or timetables of its arrival.

But these scenarios *are* to be found in Scripture. For this reason, we are not going to retreat to a Reader's Digest Bible with the troublesome parts excised. Once again, hermeneutics makes its entrance. Loving God with the mind means using the best scholarship. So the historical critic helps us to see the circumstances that surrounded the dramatic projections in Daniel and Revelation. The literary critic explores their language codes. And both, at their best, join the theological exegete to speak about larger intent easily obscured by dismissive modernity: the symbol of the antichrist and the sobriety about a closing tribulation implying a rejection of the illusion of inevitable progress; the thousand years of peace and plenty suggesting that history, for all its ambiguity, is capable of penultimate fulfillments; the role assigned to Israel—including the surprising "antisupersessionist" perspective of "pretribulational premillennialism"—reflecting the special place in Scripture and in a developing tradition of ecumenical theology assigned to God's special covenant with the Jewish people. Let us give full due to the theological meaning buried in these metaphors.[16]

But these random metaphors do not constitute an end-time metaphysics. The Scripture read canonically, ecclesially and critically fixes upon the four thats and whats we have been tracing, not the occasional and cryptic whens, wheres and hows. Through the central windows we have visions to inspire and light to read and sing, "For all the saints . . . "!

Conclusion

What was Niebuhr getting at when he said the "genius of the Christian faith" is expressed in the creedal affirmation of "the resurrection of the body"? It has to do with the heart of Christian hope.

The purposes of God are, through and through, *embodied*. God gave us bodies—personal, ecclesial, politic and cosmic. God wills their health and wholeness in the face of the corruption we and the powers and principalities have brought upon them. To that end, the very Word and Purpose of God *became* body; it became flesh. And under the assault of our crucifying no, God spoke the divine yes in the resurrection of Jesus Christ. To believe that the embodied Word rose again is to trust that the corruptibilities everywhere evident in the bodies we know—earthly and heavenly—will not have the last word. So the creed assures us in its bold words, "I believe in . . . the resurrection of the body," and through its implicit promises—the return of Christ, final judgment and everlasting life. Resurrection, Christ's and ours, is the hope by which we live and die, and the light by which we see and serve.

6

Angels Heard
& Demons Seen[†]

"ANGELS WE HAVE HEARD ON HIGH.... GLORIA IN EXCELSIS DEO!" "CHRISTIAN, dost thou see them on the holy ground, how the powers of darkness compass thee around?" In song, Scripture and stained glass, the inhabitants of an angelic "higher cosmos" and the night minions of "nothingness" are much among us. Our inquiry here will be from within this world of the pastor and teacher, the "strange new world of the Bible" never far from the local congregation.

Is that probe made easier or harder when the magazines parishioners read and the TV specials they watch feature stories of angel encounters and devil worship?[1] On the one hand, yes, easier and more inviting, for a subject too long ignored in mainline pulpits and classrooms is now breakfast talk. On the other hand, no, harder, for there is going to be a clash between the accommodating me-centered angels that fix our flat tires and Isaiah's awesome six-winged seraphim circling the throne of God.[2] At the very least, media angelology and demonology can make

[†]This essay was the introductory article for the *Theology Today* issue on angelology, vol. 51 (October 1994): 345-58.

this a moment for theological distinctions.

Today's popular interest in angels is not only the preoccupation of New Age pieties. The demythologizers, busy since the Enlightenment, are also much with us. Fiction and fantasy! And then there are the postmodern *re*mythologizers finding psychosocial meanings hidden from Enlightenment eyes. Loudest of all is the apocalyptic thunder. Graphic depictions of things to come give the New Age angels and the Satanist scenarios a good run for their money.

To clear the ground for this ecclesial inquiry, a proviso is in order:

Our reference is . . . to the Christian use of the term "angel." What has been meant and thought and written and maintained and taught in both ancient and more modern times concerning the being and existence and activity of the possible hypostases and mediators of other gods, we commit into the hands of the inventors and adherents of the relevant systems and messages and writings in which these figures occur. We are obviously unable to prevent them using the term "angel" for what they think they may know and accept and believe in this respect. We insist, however, that whatever lies to the right hand or to the left of the reality whose concept is decisively given by its relationship to the living, active and revealed God of Holy Scripture, does not correspond to the Christian idea of angel and does not deserve to be called an angel according to the Christian use . . . including . . . angels of so many mythical, spiritualistic, occult, theosophical and anthroposophical systems . . . those of popularly fantastic imagination of so many individual dreamers or whole circles of such. Nor are the beings which under this name have met with so much ridicule and skepticism and denial. . . . As Christians and theologians we must refrain from speaking of such beings as angels,

and

we must certainly not be so foolish as to try to learn from an acquaintance with such beings what is to be understood as angels in the Christian sense of the term.[3]

Karl Barth's advice is lodged within a 160-page guidebook to "the higher cosmos" of Scripture in the third volume of his *Church Dogmatics.*[4] No churchly travel over this terrain can ignore Barth and his maps. We shall be in conversation with him, following his pointing finger much of the way. But not all the way. While he is a good guide, others know some trails he has either missed or been reluctant to tread.

The Other Dimension of Creation

"Your will be done, on earth as it is in heaven." What *is* this "heaven"? The answer takes us into a doctrine of creation. The world God brought to be includes an elusive dimension. Created, but transcending our mortal coil, it is a "counterpart of the earth . . . the sum of all that which . . . is unfathomable, distant, alien and mysterious in creation."[5] Scripture has no interest in its topography (contra the long history of its map-makers), but the canonical pattern of teaching about "the kingdom of heaven" holds it to be

the Whence, the starting point, the gate from which [God] sallies with all the demonstrations and revelations and words and works of His action on earth. . . . Heaven is a place: the place of God in view of which we have to say that God is not only transcendent in relation to the world but also immanent and represented within it; the place of God from which His dealings with us, the history of the covenant, can take place in the most concrete sense, and His majesty, loftiness and remoteness can acquire the most concrete form.[6]

While little is said in Scripture about origins, a long tradition in Christian theology interprets Genesis 1:1—"In the beginning God created the heavens and the earth"—as the making of celestial as well as the terrestrial heavens and thus the creation of angels and their abode.[7] The heavenly kingdom, as the created place under the rule of God and the "whence" of the divine purposes among us, is in perfect conformity with the divine will. No surprise, then, that the biblical angels who dwell there are unswervingly obedient to the ways of God. So ordered to divine ends, they can be the "messengers of God" that their name declares, instruments among us of the purposes of heaven.

Talk of his other dimension of creation is a shock to secular contemporaries, including many Sunday worshipers on whose lips is routinely found the Lord's Prayer entreaty. A heavenly kingdom? The habitat of angels? Countersecular, yes, but the biblical narrative is incomplete without its many allusions to this invisible order of created transcendence and its agents.[8]

"Your will be done *on earth* as it is (done) in heaven." Christ prays: Let heaven's allegiances find their way to earth! The Upper Cosmos is there to show us how this world *should* work. What's there has to be communicated to what's here. Accordingly, angels in Scripture appear regularly at critical junctures of God's history with us, manifestly so at its center point—the annunciation, birth, temptations, actions, suffering, death, resurrection and ascension of Jesus Christ.

As the biblical picture of the Upper Cosmos and its relation to us begins to develop, our inclination is to hasten it along. Sharpen those lines! Give us more color! What do angels look like? How many are there? How can I get in touch with one?[9] Here Scripture is much more elusive, restrained, modest and paradoxical than our aesthetic, philosophical and cultural impulses. The Bible affords no straightforward, coherent angel ontology. We learn regularly of the *doing* of angels, but not the details of their *being*.

We know nothing of their essential being and its particular nature. We know nothing of their mutual relationship and distinction. We know nothing of the way in which they are a totality yet distinct. But we do know that even in the mystery of their being, they exist in and with the kingdom of God coming and revealed to us. . . . They are in the service of God.[10]

With even greater reserve, Barth's view of created transcendence disallows a systematic *demonology*. The "opponents of the heavenly ambassadors of God" are consigned to the regions of "nothingness" in a concluding brief discourse appended to the long investigation of angelic realities.[11] While no doctrinal locus on demons is possible, we must wonder if Reformed preoccupation with the divine sovereignty and too much talk in Heideggerian idiom of Nothingness combine in Barth's account to obscure another aspect of created— and fallen—transcendence. While the angels do belong to the fore in doctrinal explorations of Scripture's landscape, the demons must also be given their due. Creation's "lower cosmos" can describe not our plane (contra Barth), but a depth dimension of powers and principalities (contra Tillich) that have set their face against the divine purposes. After Easter, they deserve neither high profile nor equal time (contra modern apocalyptics). While not in the main body of this inquiry, we will make more than passing reference to them.

The Angel Office

What do biblical angels do? In a second-floor chapel of the sixteenth-century Antonierhaus in Bern, Switzerland, now housing a Lutheran congregation, a Fritz Pauli fresco shows an imposing angel on the ground pointing to the newborn Jesus. Here is the agent of God directing us to Another. Barth singles out this painting as more worthy than most angel art. The pointing finger, of course, is reminiscent of similar comments on Grunewald's John the Baptist.[12] Angels do not call attention to themselves but exist to witness to the Word. As noted, Scripture is not so much interested in their *nature* as in their *mission*.[13] We have no doctrine of their "person" but do learn of their "work." Angels are apertures of the divine Light. They give glimpses of the will and way of God, as that will and way comes to singular focus in Jesus Christ.

On the face of it, angels as messengers exist to execute an epistemological mission. Barth, with his focus on revelation, predictably gives angelology that turn. But the two Testaments do not limit their role to disclosure.[14] They act as well as speak. As angels that point to Christ—as angels *of Christ*—the 311 references to them in the New Testament (and, by anticipation, numerous Old Testament counterparts) can be read as a reflection of the *munus triplex* of Jesus Christ: a prophetic, priestly and royal office that accompanies and instruments Christ's own threefold work. While not taken up in conventional angelology, we pursue here the implications of a christological angelology with its threefold ministry.

Prophetic

The first office of Jesus Christ is "to be our chief Prophet and teacher, who fully reveals to us the secret counsel and will of God concerning our redemption."[15] This is the atoning work of disclosure, both then and now.[16] The angels of Christ are themselves bearers of that revelatory work, forthtelling the Word and deeds of God.

The prophetic work of angels in Scripture and tradition turns the Christian eye away from "I, me and mine." Here is an alternative understanding of God's ambassadors for pastors and teachers confronted by today's popular god-of-the-gaps spiritualities, now taking shape as angels-in-the-breach. Biblical angels are not at our beck and call. They fix our attention on God. And that attention is regularly at cross-purposes with our agenda and expectations. The prophetic ministry of Gabriel and the angelic hosts leaves no doubt about the surprise and unexpected Otherness of angel epiphanies. They inspire awe and even fear, and accordingly counsel "be not afraid." Then comes yet more of the unexpected, this time *good* news:

Greetings, favored one! The Lord is with you. . . . Do not be afraid, Mary, for you have found favor with God. And now, you will conceive in your womb and bear a son, and you will name him Jesus. (Lk 1:28, 30, 31)

Do not be afraid; for see—I am bringing you good news of great joy for all the people. (Lk 2:10)

Angels bring Good News. Not only at the beginning of the central Story, but at every turn, and at the end.

Do not be afraid. I know that you are looking for Jesus who was crucified. He is not here; for he has been raised. (Mt 28:5-6)

"Men of Galilee, why do you stand looking up toward heaven? This Jesus who has been taken from you into heaven will come in the same way as you saw him go into heaven." (Acts 1:11)

In season and out the congregation is reminded in its hymnody of the angels who brings the good word at these turning points. In well-known refrains:

Hark the herald angels sing "glory to the newborn King,
Peace on earth and mercy mild, God and sinners reconciled!"

And in less familiar ones:

An angel . . . spake unto the three, "Your Lord does go to Galilee."
(Jean Tisserand, d. 1494)

In passing, we note that hymns and liturgy keep the angelic presences before us, for as our congregations sing and say them, they instinctively employ the "divinatory imagination" Barth sees as Scripture's own way of portraying the heavenlies among us: Why should not imagination grasp real history, or the poetry which is its medium be a representation of real history, of the kind of history that escapes ordinary analogies?[17] Created transcendence makes its way into our world through saga, symbol and story, a "real history" but one requiring its own mode of discernment.

Biblical angels bring bad as well as good news. Again, sharply distinguished from today's popular angelologies, they manifest a tough as well as a tender love. Stretches of the book of Revelation challenge both our pious and secular predilections:

> The third angel poured his bowl into the rivers and the springs of water, and they became blood. And I heard the angel of the waters say, "You are just, O Holy One, who are and were, for you have judged these things." (Rev 16:4-5; cf. Rev 14—18)

Prophets tell it like it is. Likewise, the prophetic office of angels is a megaphone of the justice as well as the mercy of God.

As the prophetic office of Jesus Christ not only is exercised in Galilean ministry but is also a "continuing work," the prophetic ministry of angels is still among us. Wherever the Word of truth, justice and mercy is spoken, can the angels be far away? As Barth puts it,

> Where God is—the God who acts and reveals himself in the world created by him—heaven and the angels are also present. . . . At bottom a piety or theology in which there is no mystery, which lacks the mirror of self-representing deity, and in which there are therefore no angels, will surely prove to be a godless theology.[18]

Priestly

> And suddenly there was with the angel a multitude of the heavenly host, praising God and saying, "Glory to God in the highest heaven, and on earth peace among those whom he favors!" (Lk 2:13-14)

With angelic news comes angelic praise. Once again, biblical angels are pointers to Another, this time "practicing what they preach." And again, good hymnody and liturgy may keep our theology on track when our preaching and teaching wander and falter. What congregation rightly ordered has not had some hint of this office in its opening act of worship when it has joined the angels in adoration, singing

> Holy, holy, holy, Lord God Almighty! . . .
> Cherubim and seraphim falling down before thee.

The priestly office of Jesus Christ in Reformation confession and catechism is to make sacrifice: the eternal Son of God suffering and dying for the sins of the world. The Reformers saw this office carried forward in the body of Christ on earth in the priesthood of all believers who "make a living sacrifice of thankfulness to Him."[19] The angels of Scripture as messengers of God model this "sacrifice of praise and thanksgiving":

> In the year that King Uzziah died, I saw the Lord sitting on a throne, high and lofty; and the hem of his robe filled the temple. Seraphs were in attendance above him. . . . And one called to another and said:
>
> "Holy, holy, holy, is the LORD of hosts;
> the whole earth is full of his glory." (Is 6:1-3)

Isaiah's angels teach us the heart of worship: not our issues and our needs to the fore, but the glory of God.

Leander Keck in his recent Beecher lectures, *The Church Confident,* charges mainline churches with the loss of the biblical praise of God, it being "displaced by anthropocentric utilitarianism."[20] Interests that run from the therapeutic to the political have so intruded themselves into our Sunday services that the "theocentrism" of Isaiah's temple has disappeared.

> If praise is the heart of worship, then making worship useful destroys it, because it introduces an ulterior motive for praise. And ulterior motives mean manipulation, taking charge of the relationship, thereby turning the relation between the Creator and creature upside down. In this inversion, the living God, whose biblical qualities like jealousy and wrath have been tamed, has been deprived of freedom, having been reduced to the Great Enabler, now has little to do but warrant our causes and help us fulfill our aspirations. . . . The opening line of the Westminster Confession is now reversed, for the chief end of God is to glorify us and to be useful to us indefinitely.[21]

The charge of reversal—glorifying ourselves rather than God—is not limited to mainline churches, for evangelical David Wells has indicted modern evangelicalism for the same anthropocentrism.[22] Can the angels teach us, once again, what it means to praise God? Not those of pop culture. The reports of their presence have consistently to do with their usefulness to our needs and wishes (see Keck and

Wells above). On the other hand, biblical angels have a priestly office, a psalmic turning of the eye of faith in the direction of the divine glory. In liturgical worship the praise of God reaches a stirring climax in eucharistic prayer and seraphic hymn:

> Thee mighty God . . . we magnify and praise. With apostles and martyrs . . . with the innumerable company of angels round about thy throne, the heaven of heavens and all the powers therein, we worship and adore they glorious Name, joining in the song of the Seraphim and Cherubim—"Holy, Holy, Holy, Lord God of Sabaoth, heaven and earth are full of thy glory. . . . Hosanna in the highest!"[23]

To join the angels in that ascent is to be taught by their priesting work.

Royal

Christ the King, according to the Heidelberg catechism, "governs us by his word and Spirit, and defends and preserves us in the redemption obtained for us."[24] The royal office of angels is executed in kind. Angels save Lot and his family from destruction (Gen 19:1-19), protect Daniel in the lions' den (Dan 6:23), care for Jesus after his temptations (Mt 4:11) and strengthen him in the garden (Lk 22:43). They are, throughout the Bible, "ministering spirits" (Heb 1:14). Angels do deeds as well as praise God and bring news.

Does the royal office sound a little like Sophy Burnham's "reflections on angels . . . and true stories of how they touch our lives"?[25] Some crucial distinctions are in order:

1. Biblical angels are about God's business. In each case, beneficent Powers are released to accomplish something integral to the divine purposes. All actions comport with and contribute to that end. Read christologically, these deeds are under Christ's regency and testify to his truth. The critical test all claims to angel visitation must pass is: Do they serve the realm of God and testify to Jesus Christ?

2. As part of a threefold office, the angelic act is never separable from angelic Word and worship. The deed done carries with it the expectation of hearing the Word and making the act of thanksgiving. Is a life changed, a truth gained, God praised? Is the act of deliverance accompanied by a new will "to deny oneself" and "to take up the cross"?

3. Popular testimonies to angel aid speak regularly of one's "guard-

ian angel," or rescue by a single supernal being. Of the hundreds of biblical allusions to angels, only two references to individual guardianship appear: Job 33:23 and Acts 12:15. Neither requires a theory of full-time oversight. And a canonical hermeneutic would not build an angelology—or any ology—on such slender evidence.

To challenge the narcissism of New Age angelology is not to deny the *present* deed-doing ministry of beneficent powers. As the angels still speak the Word and praise the Lord, they continue with us also as ministering spirits. But biblical sobriety calls us to "test the spirits to see whether they are from God" (1 Jn 4:1), as in the above scrutiny. Yet Scripture, as judicious as it is, in another sense is more exuberant about angel presences than most modern claimants. Here the always sober Calvin has a surprise for us. Guardian angels? Why settle for *one?* There are *hosts* about us.

> We ought to hold as a fact that the care of each one of us is not the task of one angel only, but all with one consent watch over our salvation. . . . For if the fact that all the heavenly host are keeping watch for his safety will not satisfy a man, I do not see what benefit he could derive from knowing that one angel has been given to him as his especial guardian.[26]

And of a piece with this challenge to individualistic preoccupations is the Reformer's wariness of personal hoverings diverting attention from the real Source:

> Thus it happens that what belongs to God and Christ alone is transferred to them. . . . Even John in Revelation confesses that this happened to him, but at the same time he adds . . . "You must not do that! . . . Worship God."[27]

Angel Experiences and Realities

Popular angelologies revel in angel experiences. In contrast, Martin Luther prayed that he would not meet one. St. Paul rarely talked about them in his letters. Whole stretches of Scripture have nothing to say about them. Hymnody helps again to put things in perspective:

> I ask no dream, no prophet ecstasies . . . no angel visitant, no opening skies.

Why this reserve? Surely it has to do with the believer's experience of *God.* For Christians, over time, the divine encounter has had to do with pneumatology, not angelology. The richness of meeting Jesus Christ by the power of the Holy Spirit empties the soul of all craving for angel visitations. Is a culture devoid of classical piety fertile soil for the claims of other encounters?

The account of Abraham's meeting with the three strangers in Genesis 19:1-20 suggests another reason for experiential modesty. The visitation had to do with three travelers welcomed to the table, not winged creatures of supernatural appearance. Only after their departure did Abraham realize he had entertained "angels un-awares." Angel epiphanies in Scripture regularly take place in earthy and ordinary circumstances. They require the gift of discernment. Their presence is empirical but not experiential, embodied in our space and time, but not self-evidently so.

The angels keep their ancient places—
Turn but a stone and start a wing!
'Tis ye, 'tis ye, your estranged faces
That miss the many-splendoured thing.[28]

Here the studies of Walter Wink make an important contribution to the theological discernment of the powers among us. In his trilogy, *Naming the Powers, Unmasking the Powers* and *Engaging the Powers,* careful exegetical work and insightful psychosocial analysis combine to give us one contemporary understanding of Scripture's references to *exousia, archai, dynameis, thronos, kyriotes, angelos.*[29] Finding these terms fluid and largely interchangeable, he argues that they refer not to

> separate heavenly or ethereal entities but . . . the *inner aspect of material or tangible manifestations of Power.* I suggest that the "principalities and powers" are the inner or spiritual essence, or gestalt, of an institution or state or system. . . . "The Powers" should no longer be reserved for the special category of spiritual forces, but should rather be used generically for all manifestations of power, seen under the dual aspect of their physical or institutional concretion, on the one hand, and their inner essence or spiritual-ity on the other.[30]

Wink makes a persuasive case that New Testament allusions to "powers and principalities," "thrones" and "authorities" can be understood to be spiritual dynamisms associated with experienced phenomena, the institutions and forces of our day-to-day world.

Wink's insights have enabled clergy better to understand peculiar forces alive in the church as institution, the "angels" of the congregations in which we live and work. They are data for a "theology of institutions" shedding light for laity on the meaning of their workplace as an "authority" that is both a locus for their secular ministry and a "power" called to its own ministry.[31] In the present context, they represent the "underside" of biblical angelology. Human life, in this case in its institutional expression, is the medium through which the angels come among us "unawares." Indeed, they do so for ill as well as good, a topic to which we shall subsequently turn.

Wink's interpretation of the human and institutional expression of angelic powers, however, must be related to the larger threefold office. As such, his proposal to interpret biblical angelology only in terms of psychosocial and institutional dynamics must be challenged as reductionist. Biblical powers are for telling and praising as well as institutional "doing." And the mysterious More of the Scripture's "ethereal entities" cannot be reduced to the plausibilities of critical analysis.[32]

The tracing of the threefold "work" of angels in Scripture also poses the postmodern question: Are we drawing a picture of the biblical cosmos and sketching in some often neglected characters? Is this a storybook world into which we invite the reader, one with its own countercultural expectations and demands juxtaposed to society's values? Yes. But no to the sometimes assumed corollary that no claims can be made for the correspondence of this narrative to real states of affairs. The Upper Cosmos is not a fictive realm. Biblical ontology, while modest, is not missing. Angels are true messengers of a true God. They can no more be reduced to the stories of postmodernity than to the institutions of modernity. This is a world "strange" to cultural categories. Accounts of the angelic legions do conform to the "real order" of things.

Dealing with the Demons

Both Satanist cults and "post-trib pre-mils" have much to say about the immediate regency of dark powers. Ironically, the extremes meet in their mesmerism with evil. Again, the ideologies of the hour—very different here from the sunnier New Ageisms—make for a teaching moment, this time on the "fallen angels."

The biblical story does, indeed, speak about tempters and seducers at its beginning, middle and culmination. The world did fall away from the divine purpose (Eden, understood theologically as the divine intention for creation), carrying down with it elements of a good created transcendence. In Christian tradition, more is said about Satan than any leading angelic counterpart. And in the earlier twentieth-century recovery of a biblical theology of powers and principalities, with its background struggle against modern isms, the emphasis has been on "rebellious powers."[33] The demonic is more remarked upon than the angelic, as in Tillichian analysis[34] and Niebuhrian realism about "immoral society."[35] The popularity of C. S. Lewis's *Screwtape Letters* is yet another testimony to the power of the Christian imagination in our troubled time.[36]

Sobriety, sensitivity to the dark side, realism, yes. However, they have to do with penultimate, not ultimate, reality. Luther, who was no stranger to such struggles, left us the reminder of that finality:

The prince of darkness grim, we tremble not for him;

His rage we can endure, for lo, his doom is sure:

One little word shall fell him.

Although we confront a "world with devils filled," the enemy has met its match:

He disarmed the rulers and authorities and made a public example of them, triumphing over them. (Col 2:15)

Because Christ "made captivity . . . captive" (Eph 4:8), we do not tremble at the saber-rattling of the powers.

In his memorable *Letter to Great Britain,* with bombs falling on London, Barth echoed this powerful "because . . . therefore."

The world in which we live is the place where Jesus Christ rose from the dead. . . . Since this is true [it] is not some sinister wilderness where fate or chance hold sway or where all sorts of "principalities and powers" run riot unrestrained and range about unchecked. . . . We Christians . . . have no right whatsoever to fear or respect them or resign ourselves to the fact that they are spreading throughout the world as though they knew neither bounds nor lord. We should be slighting the resurrection of Jesus Christ and denying his reign on the right hand of the Father, if we forget that the world in which we live is already consecrated, and if we did not, for Christ's sake, come to grips spiritedly with these evil spirits, and smite them.[37]

To the young who flirt with the satanic and the old fearful of the demonic, the message is: "Be not afraid." The Christ to whom the angels point rules even these ominous powers. They should worry about us with our "one little Word," not the other way around. For all its peculiarities and popular distortions, the rite of exorcism practiced in some Christian traditions is rooted in this conviction of the regency of Jesus Christ. And that same trust in the royal office of Christ (and the angels) fortifies us in the struggle against political, economic and social powers as real in our time as in other eras.

But now comes the Enlightenment caveat: "Along with all the high theology, Luther hurled an ink pot at the devil. Are you inviting us back into this precritical world?" Wink's studies take this question seriously but invite the critic forward into post-Enlightenment times, ones that are able to appreciate at least the experiential underside of the biblical realm of thrones and authorities. Scripture speaks of discussable realities that make their presence known in our historical and personal tumults.

The damaging work of rebellious powers looks a lot like the reverse of the royal office of the angels: done deeds of bondage not deliverance. Do the demons have their own threefold office? In Scripture there seem to be false prophets of the Upper Cosmos that bring bad news and untruth and fallen priests that blaspheme. Are the heirs today of the "father of lies" (Jn 8:44) the prophets of institutional untruth and the false priestcraft in the cult of corporations that demands sacrifice rather than offers it?

To name the spirituality of institutions in the language of Scripture has an apologetic force, especially for those at home in metaphor, symbol and story. But as with angels so with demons: we cannot reduce the biblical characters to our conventions. There is a More here in things demonic. What that More is takes us to questions beyond "mission" to "nature." But again we meet with biblical reserve about angels fallen as well as unfallen, giving us no clear ontology of the demonic. And why would there be if Satan has already fallen (Lk 10:18) and Jesus has already led captivity captive?

There seems to be a correlation between those with elaborate descriptions of the demons and the devil and the belief that the latter are now in charge; again the cultists and the apocalyptics join forces.[38] While the Story tells us that we struggle with evil until the End, that End has already begun, the enemy already having been dealt a mortal wound:

The Old Dragon under ground,

In straiter limits bound,

Not half so far casts his usurped sway,

And, wroth to see his Kingdom fall,

Swinges the scaly horror of his folded tail.[39]

Metaphor here serves better than metaphysics. And with it mission: exorcising the remnants of demonic presence wherever they appear in the arrogance of institutional power or the subtler temptations and seductions of the soul.

Conclusion

We began with our sanctuaries and congregations, and end there. Much soul-searching goes on these days about what transpires in our pews and pulpits. Have the seductions of culture emptied the former and eroded the message of the latter? It's no accident that Barmen's call to listen to "the one Word of God . . . Jesus Christ as he is attested to us in Holy Scripture" is now increasingly heard as a challenge to the church's acculturation. With it we should remember the words of the author of Barmen quoted earlier, that "a piety or theology in which there is no mystery . . . no angels . . . is a godless theology." The work of Christ in Scripture is inseparable from the work of angels.

For all that, biblical angels are on the edge, not the center, of Christian faith, in the stained-glass windows but not on the altar. That they *are* very much there in our songs, texts and sanctuaries should give us, as too often forgetful teachers and preachers, some pause. Their prophetic, priestly and royal work under and for Jesus Christ have made a difference in the life and witness of other generations. And not to remember the demonic counterparts to the angelic hosts is the best assist we can give to the agents of Nothingness. In recentering in Jesus Christ, may we better see the demons lurking and hear the angels singing.

Part III
Ecumenical &
Evangelical Explorations

---

*This section examines theological writings that reflect
end-of-century trends, ecumenical and evangelical. The first
essay is a review of representative works in the surge in
systematics, with some early 1990s history of the new
flourishing of this field. The following two chapters both
describe and critique developments in the expanding world of
evangelicalism. The final chapter describes a new and more
modest ecumenism of both affirmation and admonition.*

7

In Quest of the Comprehensive[†]

The Systematics Revival

Evans, James H., Jr. *We Have Been Believers: An African-American Theology*. Minneapolis: Fortress, 1992; Jewett, Paul K. *God, Creation and Revelation: A Neo-evangelical Theology*. With Sermons by Marguerite Shuster. Grand Rapids, Mich.: Eerdmans, 1991; Migliore, Daniel L. *Faith Seeking Understanding: An Introduction to Christian Theology*. Grand Rapids, Mich.: Eerdmans, 1991; Neville, Robert Cummings. *A Theology Primer*. Albany: State University of New York Press, 1991; Peters, Ted. *God—the World's Future: Systematic Theology for a Postmodern Era*. Minneapolis: Fortress, 1992; Smart, Ninian, and Steven Konstantine. *Christian Systematic Theology in a World Context*. Minneapolis: Fortress, 1991; Sölle, Dorothee. *Thinking About God: An Introduction to Theology*. London: SCM Press, and Philadelphia: Trinity Press International, 1990.

"IS SYSTEMATIC OR CONSTRUCTIVE THEOLOGY POSSIBLE IN OUR TIME?" THIS query from the editor of *Religious Studies Review* has been answered by a chorus of noes from the ad hoc advocates of the secular sixties to the latter-day proponents of postmodern ambiguity. Theologians paid attention to this counsel for some time, with a few exceptions. But now a rebellion is afoot. We are in the midst of a remarkable outpouring of works variously described as "introductions," "systematics" or "dogmatics" that cover from a stated point of view most or all of the standard loci.

Our question will be answered here descriptively and normatively. Yes, many self-defined works in this genre *are* being written

---

[†]This essay was based on an article with the same title in *Religious Studies Review* 20 (January 1994): 7-12.

today. Hence, a brief history of the phenomenon is in order. But do they qualify as systematic/constructive theology? Our *seven* designated volumes—to the extent that they are representative of the larger development—are test cases of its "possibility" in the normative sense.

Retrieval and Reconstruction

Two very different figures and frameworks indicate the character and direction of the current systematics revival: Gustavo Gutiérrez and Carl Henry. Their major works, conceived or written in the early seventies (neither of which is described as systematics), are forerunners of the current phenomenon: *A Theology of Liberation* and *God, Revelation and Authority.* (A case could be made that James Cone's 1970 *Black Theology of Liberation* preceded both of these, but the nature and brevity of its topical analysis keeps it short of the "comprehensive" characteristic of a systematics to be noted below.) The point of entry for both is theological method and "religious epistemology," the neuralgic issues of the period. Yet they move beyond these to traverse and integrate the doctrinal commonplaces. Each understands itself as *a* "theology," but in contrast to the recent flurry of such self-identified movements they are theologies "in the round," interpreting most of the standard teachings of the church. Henry and Gutiérrez also anticipate the two poles of systematics-to-come, ones suggested by the editorial nomenclature ("systematics or constructive theology"): (1) retrieval of a tradition overwhelmed by the *Zeitgeist* (Henry); (2) reconstruction of the tradition in response to new or denied contexts (Gutiérrez).

On the heels of these anticipatory ventures—in the late seventies to mid-eighties—the first wave of self-conscious systematics/dogmatics/constructive theology made its appearance. Among the authors were "retrievalists," especially those of evangelical persuasion: Donald Bloesch, *Essentials of Evangelical Theology;* Millard Erickson, *Christian Theology;* and James Montgomery Boice's revised *Christian Faith.* Others were "reconstructionists," rebuilding the house of doctrine from the ground up: Paul van Buren, beginning a three-volume series restating historic teaching, post-Holocaust, and in the light of "Jewish-Christian reality"; Rosemary Radford Ruether, *Sexism and God-Talk,* reframing the loci in feminist perspective; Marjorie Hewitt Suchocki, *God-Christ-Church,* restating key themes from within a process framework; Fred Herzog, *God-Walk,* calling for a liberation reading of standard topics for a North American context. Others concerned to retrieve the tradition yet relate to the context spoke more of "reinterpretation," in a self-identified ecumenical way: Geoffrey Wainwright, *Doxology;* Hendrikus Berkhof, *Christian Faith;* Jan Lochman, *The Faith We Confess;* Otto Weber, *Foundations of Dogmatics;* Helmut Thielicke, *The Evangelical Faith;* Owen Thomas, *Introduction to Theology;* Langdon Gilkey, *Message and Existence;* and the writer's *The Christian Story.* Collections as well as individual authors were part of this scene, with participants sharing some common assumptions but developing individual topics from different points of view: Peter Hodgson and Robert King, eds., *Christian Theology: An Introduction to Its Traditions and Tasks;* Carl Braaten and Robert Jenson, eds., *Christian Dogmatics.*

Some of the systematics attempted in this initial phase were, to one degree or another, written from within a specific church tradition: Braaten and Jenson's volumes and Hans Schwarz, *Responsible Faith*— Lutheran; Karl Rahner, *Foundations of Christian Faith,* and Richard McBrien, *Catholicism*—Roman Catholic; Dwight Moody, *The Word of Truth,* James McClendon's first volume, *Ethics,* and Kenneth Cauthen, *Systematic Theology*—varieties of Baptist tradition; A. T. Hanson and R. P. C. Hanson's *Reasonable Belief*—Anglican.

From the end of the decade to the present, the number of systematics projects has dramatically increased. Evangelicals continue to be prominent in the move to recover traditional teachings, often with detailed critiques of other options: Gordon Lewis and Bruce Demarest, *Integrative Theology;* James Leo Garrett Jr., *Systematic Theology;* Robert Lightner, *Evangelical Theology;* Alan F. Johnson and Robert E. Webber, *What Christians Believe: A Biblical and Historical Summary;* Wayne Grudem, *Systematic Theology;* Stanley Grenz, *Theology for the Community of God;* Paul Jewett, *Neo-evangelical Theology* volumes. Donald Bloesch is in the fourth of a seven-volume series published by InterVarsity Press (Christian Foundations). InterVarsity has also begun a nine-volume series, Contours of Christian Theology, edited by Gerald Bray. British evangelical Alister McGrath has written for Blackwell the university-oriented *Christian Theology: An Introduction,* and has on the docket a two-volume work in systematics. Thomas Oden joins the retrievalists as "paleo-orthodox" in a three-volume systematic theology (*The Living God, The Word of Life* and *Life in the Spirit*).

The collection edited by Susan Brooks Thistlethwaite and Mary Potter Engel, *Lift Every Voice*, takes a decided reconstructionist turn with feminist, liberation and multicultural accents. In the same vein is Rebecca S. Chopp and Mark Lewis Taylor, editors of *Reconstructing Christian Theology*. So too Gordon Kaufman, as he abandons his earlier "systematics" self-definition for *In the Face of Mystery*, an open-ended "constructive theology." Peter Hodgson (coeditor of the widely used earlier-mentioned work) gives pride of place to context in *Winds of the Spirit*.

Retrieving the tradition but giving attention as well to context (North America) are Douglas Hall's three-volume *Thinking the Faith, Professing the Faith* and *Confessing the Faith*. Christopher Morse's *Not Every Spirit: A Dogmatics of Christian Disbelief* also actively relates classical texts to contemporary issues. Justo González argues the relevance of Chalcedonian Christology to the plight of the poor in *Mañana: Christian Theology from a Hispanic Perspective*. Against the backdrop of Lesslie Newbigin's "gospel and culture" emphasis is Hugh Montefiore's *Credible Christianity: The Gospel in Contemporary Society*. Robert Jenson's two-volume *Systematic Theology* is a retrievalist work, but in running dialogue with contemporary ecclesial and cultural contexts.

Earlier ecclesial emphases are now in full voice: Francis Schüssler Fiorenza and John Galvin's edited collection *Systematic Theology*, and the inception of Frans Josef van Beeck's series *God Encountered*—Roman Catholic; Thomas Finger, *Christian Theology*—eschatologically oriented Mennonite themes; Gordon Spykman, *Reformational Theology*—Christian Reformed; John H. Leith, *Basic Christian Doctrine*—Reformed; Shirley C. Guthrie, *Christian Doctrine*, revised edition—Reformed; J. Rodney Williams, *Renewal Theology*, a three-volume systematics "in charismatic perspective"; Richard Rice, *The Reign of God*, systematics "from a Seventh-Day Adventist perspective"; Ray Dunning, *Grace, Faith and Holiness*—"a Wesleyan systematic theology" in the Nazarene tradition. William W. Menzies and Stanley M. Horton have written *Bible Doctrines—A Pentecostal Perspective*. A. J. Conyers, *A Basic Christian Theology*, and the earlier-mentioned Grenz work are in the Baptist tradition. Michael Pomazansky offers *Orthodox Dogmatic Theology*.

Two theologians whose reputations as well as the extent of their systematics ventures place them in a class of their own are Wolfhart Pannenberg and Jürgen Moltmann. All three volumes of Pannenberg's *Systematic Theology* are now available in English, as is Moltmann's five-volume systematics series, *Messianic Theology*.

In Jewish thought, Eugene Borowitz has pioneered "a systematic statement" in *Renewing the Covenant: A Theology for the Postmodern Jew.*

Our Sample Considered

While the answer to the doability of systematics is, empirically, yes, we have yet to address the question in terms of legitimacy and viability. Among the various ways to make this judgment—cultural aptness (a needed "new paradigm"?), ecclesial timeliness, consonance with one's own point of view, etc.—our test here will be classics in the field. We measure the current output not against the extent or depth of classical literature but by its key features. Thus comprehensive and integrative works of systematic/constructive theology (however labeled)—such as those of Origen, Aquinas, Calvin, Schleiermacher and Barth—are characterized by (1) "indwelling" (Polanyi) the tradition, immersion in and knowledge about the theological heritage; (2) engaging culture with imagination and integrity, sensitivity to its issues, facility with its idiom; (3) thoroughness in the treatment of topics; (4) conversation with the community and knowledgeability of and dialogue with its diverse constituencies. Systematics/constructive theology is normatively possible, whatever its point of view or its place in the retrieval, reinterpretation and reconstruction spectrum employed earlier, to the extent that it embodies these characteristics.

Indwelling the Tradition

All the authors affirm the importance of the ancient landmarks, of Scripture and the official sedimentations of doctrine. They also acknowledge the importance of the long history of theological debate and its exemplary figures and show acquaintance with the matrices of liturgy, piety and mission. The degree to which acknowledgment and acquaintance evidences indwelling varies greatly.

Paul Jewett makes an extensive case for the authority of Scripture and warrants his positions by frequent textual citation and occasional exegesis (with a biblical index of over a thousand references). He makes a long hermeneutical discussion with special attention to intraevangelical disputes, expounding his own christological cum "infallibilist" hermeneutic (contra inerrancy—"free from . . . finespun redundancies and . . . hermeneutical games" [Jewett, 131]), as it is grounded in a nuanced doctrine of verbal inspiration and personal illumination (Calvin so cited), one that allows for modest uses of critical scholarship. He regularly cites the works of Aquinas, Augustine, Calvin, Luther and Schleiermacher, shows familiarity with the Greek fathers and cites creedal and confessional texts. Predictably, for the single evangelical theologian in our list (the proportions in the larger systematics phenomenon are much greater), the indwelling of Scripture is of highest importance.

Daniel Migliore and Ted Peters can be partnered in the character and weighting of elements in the tradition. They join Jewett in the avowal of *suprema scriptura* but attend more actively in its interpretation to their respective ecclesial heritages—Migliore, Reformed, and Peters, Lutheran. Migliore, showing the influence of Barth, cites Scripture frequently and reads it christologically but also contextually, stressing the hermeneutical privilege of the victim and sensitivity to liberation and ecological movements. "The sociality of God" (Migliore, 69) is a refrain that reflects Migliore's frequent conjunction of tradition and mission. Scripture for Peters is the "criterial source and formal norm" of systematics and is regularly referenced. The gospel—Luther's *Christum treiben*—is its material norm, with "justification," "new creation" and "proclamation" as interpretive keys (Peters, 46-51). Peters stresses more than Migliore or Jewett the inseparability of Scripture and the church, with the ecclesial work of the Spirit validating the canon. With Migliore, he reads Scripture with an eye to its socioeconomic significance, but treats as principal interlocutor the postmodern mind in its scientific, literary and cultural manifestations. Both Migliore and Peters reject theories of biblical inspiration, associating them with biblicism and fundamentalism; they argue for the importance but not the control of critical scholarship and express trust in the present work of the Spirit to make the Word alive in the church.

Sölle speaks of "three elements which govern systematic theology": "the text" (Scripture and tradition), "the context" (the historical situation) and the community of believers (Sölle, 3), paralleling three of our rubrics here. Juxtaposing her own liberation hermeneutic to "orthodox" and "liberal" approaches (this typology is used in the discussion of each topic), she argues for a "social criticism" of biblical and ecclesial texts, with its premise of "the hermeneutical privilege of the oppressed" (Sölle, 69). In the treatment of systematics topics this means an underscoring of the social significance of traditional teaching (the ecological implications of the doctrine of creation), the challenge of past reductionist readings (only personal and no systemic sin and grace), the stress needed in our context (participation in the sufferings of Christ among the poor). Scripture is cited frequently and always in the setting of social struggles, from Germany and the United States to Latin America and South Africa. Reference is regularly made to church tradition with appended cautions: "the exaggerated and steep christology of the tradition" (Sölle, 115) eliminates the real humanity of Jesus and lacks connection with living issues.

For Evans the Bible is "a plumb line for the life and practice of the Christian community" (Evans, 33) because it is "the record of God's revelation to humanity" (Evans, 27). However, its use by slave holders to justify their abhorrent conduct (the "Hamitic curse," for example) means that African-American Christians have read it, and today must read it, "in the context of the struggle for liberation" (Evans, 40). The contextual lens so formed is shaped by "the traditions of African-American worshipping congregations, African-American culture and the African-American worldview" (Evans, 27). Drawing on his studies in literary theory (Robert Alter, Erich Auerbach, Frank Kermode et al.) as well as the historic practice of black church preaching and worship, Evans argues for an "indeterminacy of meaning in the text" (Evans, 46) inviting imaginative interpretation—"conjuring"—that joins the biblical narrative to the personal and social stories of the African-American freedom struggle.

Neville uses the "Methodist quadrilateral"—Scripture, tradition, reason and experience—but unlike the espousal of scriptural primacy in Wesley and official Methodism, "allows each to be a critical interpreter and appraiser of the others" (Neville, 13). Biblical allusions are sparse, and there is no discussion of interpretive principles comparable to Migliore, Peters, Sölle, Evans and Jewett, although "the mind of Christ"

(Neville, 154) is a formula appearing throughout, as set within the refrain of "covenant." The historic specifics of the various doctrines are treated briefly, with the weight on their philosophical reconstruction in a modified process mode around the theme of Logos as "form, components of form, their actual mixture, and value" (Neville, 45). Neville appends to each chapter a listing of alternative readings on a given topic by notables in classical theology (Aquinas, Augustine, Calvin, Luther, Hildegaard of Bingen, Schleiermacher) along with important twentieth-century writers (Barth, Cobb and Griffin, Rahner, Tillich, Ruether), but does not discuss them.

Ninian Smart and Steven Konstantine, self-conscious about their respective Anglican and Eastern Orthodox identities, affirm the range of tradition as we have defined it, including Scripture, official doctrinal formulas in some cases, historic theological discussion (especially patristic figures) and the liturgical and artistic riches of the church. The Bible, however, is "at best only part of the substance of actual Christian worldviews" (Smart and Konstantine, 86), supplemented by "the life of the community"—especially its heroes and saints (Smart and Konstantine, 99), to be read with critical apparatus and the critical consciousness of liberation movements, but more so in "the whole-world context, and the reflection of that in religious studies" (Smart and Konstantine, 17). Classical teaching about the Trinity, atonement and the Eucharist in particular is discussed, with each interpreted in the framework of a "neo-transcendentalism" and "soft non-relativism" that locates the specifics of Christian teaching as an arguable, but finally "adaptive," variation on a universally known and saving Reality. The exposition of each subject makes little use of Scripture.

With due regard to the varying length of their works, the attention to the tradition by Jewett, Migliore, Peters and Sölle is serious, that of Smart and Konstantine selective, that of Neville random. Students using the first four as systematics texts, and others looking for the theological trajectories from the past, would be given a respectful introduction to the historic reference points, albeit from perspectives as diverse as evangelical, liberation and "postmodern." They would be well served by Smart and Konstantine with respect to the "divine threefoldedness" (fifty pages of imaginative reconstruction by Konstantine of patristic and contemporary thought on the social Trinity) and Neville on sanctification, but not given significant access to the heritage in other respects by these authors.

Engaging Culture

As indicated in the foregoing, the cultural profile is much higher in some of these works than in others. Readers of Smart and Konstantine are plunged into a religiously pluralistic world, and find their way in it with the aid of Smart's extensive studies in the field and Konstantine's ambitious chart of the interrelationships and commonalities of major world religions (Smart and Konstantine, 52-53). Neville joins them in accenting the importance of world religions. He is sensitive to feminist issues and stresses current ecological and justice concerns, but also provides philosophical clarifications of the contextualizing process based on his own previous work: "a contemporary way of describing truth is to say that it is a carryover into the interpreter's experience of the value of things interpreted, as qualified by the special limitations of the interpreter's physical being, culture, symbol system, and purposes" (Neville, 9).

Sölle's perspective is deeply marked by feminist and Third World liberation movements and by peace and ecology issues. Thus the conviction that the cultural interlocutor is today's victim rather than modernity's philosophical doubter or religious seeker. Poignant stories of suffering and social struggle are frequently part of the exposition of a topic. Migliore sounds some of the same notes, but with less experiential underpinning and more connection to classical Reformed themes and doctrinal elaboration. He also brings his liberation framework to all the standard loci, in contrast to Sölle's more selective coverage. Peters deals extensively with feminist critiques but is less sympathetic to them than Sölle or Migliore. Literary and scientific developments and the challenges of religious pluralism figure prominently in his reinterpretations, with a Pannenbergian "futurity" serving as organizing principle.

As noted, Evans holds the interpretation of Scripture to be inextricable from cultural matrices, in both oppressive and liberating ways, past and present. For example, in the positive and historic senses, African culture provided slaves with the framework of the "traditional African heroic epic" (Evans, 82) that enabled them to make a "figural" appropriation of the mediatorial work of Christ. Today a vigorous "nascent black theology," one that includes womanist and African as well as high-profile North American male theologians, is shaping a point of view that continues and enriches earlier exodus (liberation) and Ethiopic (cultural) models.

Jewett shows acquaintance with feminist literature and expresses sympathy with its struggle against patriarchy. In a notable departure from all the other systematics here considered, he employs *her* as the only pronoun for God in a 110-page treatment of the divine attributes (using a balancing *him* in other sections [Smart and Konstantine use *her* for God throughout]) and incorporates homilies from a woman pastor (Marguerite Shuster) in the articulation of each doctrine. Beyond this specific concern, however, there is little exposure of the reader to the cultural challenges addressed by the other works.

The diversity of cultural conversation partners distinguishes these endeavors from classical systematics, which tend to engage the overarching systems or underlying premises of their times. In this respect, current works reflect the pluralism of our period and cannot impose a homogeneity where there is none. Most do creative reinterpretation of the tradition in terms of one or another cultural challenge. Ventures that probe the specifics of religious pluralism, systemic oppression and ecological peril or employ analytical tools of literary, scientific or philosophical provenance are to be commended. However, systematics by its very nature resists reductionism. Can cultural engagement be limited to one or another interlocutor? The comprehensive is here elusive.

Topical Inclusivity and Integration

Systematics, by definition, is a venture in comprehensiveness, visiting the standard locations of Christian teaching and showing how they relate to one another. The adequacy of a work must therefore be measured by how thoroughly the trek is made from an introductory discussion of definitions and methodology to content issues of creation and Fall, person and work, church, salvation, consummation and the doctrine of God that emerges therefrom. Inclusivity and coherence of this sort also have their practical consequences, as factors in the suitability of a book as an introductory course text. The brevity of a given work makes this journey more difficult; but some of the volumes in this sampling, and others in the longer list, show that is doable.

While among the shorter works, Migliore's volume successfully covers the loci. "The sociality of God" (69) as exegeted in Reformed fashion with liberation accents provides an integrating theme throughout. Peters's longer systematics also deals with all the standard subjects, going into more detail than others in our sample on Christology and ecclesiology, with Pannenberg's "retroactive ontology" (224) as organizing principle.

Smart and Konstantine have written the longest but the least topically comprehensive single volume of the seven under consideration. While the Trinity is given prominence and important aspects of Christology and ecclesiology are addressed, the world religions cum the authors' social-science interests leave little space for methodical examination of other loci. A "pluralist, social Trinitarian, universalist panentheism" (441) integrates the subjects treated.

The shortest volumes, by Sölle, Evans and Neville, have to work hard to cover the standard topics. Sölle comes closest to this goal with her discussion of authority in various perspectives—creation, sin and grace, Christ, the kingdom of God and the church, and the doctrine of God. However, the format of comparing at each juncture orthodox, liberal and liberation paradigms, and the separate essays on feminist and black theologies and a theology of peace—all of which effectively develop her framework—also delimit the seriousness with which the standard topics can be addressed. After a major section on theological method, Evans takes up in turn the doctrines of God, Christ, humanity, church and the future—ultimate and penultimate, with fugitive references to sin or salvation, but no sections on these subjects per se. The treatment of each selected topic focuses on the slice of historic teaching that connects with the author's interpretation of the African-American agenda (theodicy and the divine personality in the doctrine of God; humanity as created for freedom in anthropology: liberation as "what the church is" [Evans, 135], not only what it does in ecclesiology) but often omits long-standing dimensions and discussions of the loci. Neville's chapters deal with many of the loci, although ordered somewhat differently (the nature of theology, revelation, God as Creator, Trinity, the human condition—covenant and sin, salvation, justification, sin and society, sanctification, Christology, the Holy Spirit and the church). The reader will be instructed by the treatment of "God as Creator," of Christology and sanctification, especially in their philosophical import, but will find the other topics undeveloped. Sölle and Neville do not have chapters on eschatology.

No comparative measure can be made of Jewett's work; his volume was intended as the first of a series, a project foreshortened by the author's death (although the publisher is considering a sequel based on class notes). The exposition of the three subjects undertaken— God, creation and revelation—is extensive, as might be expected in a 535-page work on three loci, integrated according to a "neo-evangelical" point of view.

All the works under review are clear about their organizing principles and integrate their subject matter in the light of them. The diversity of frameworks is striking. Topical inclusivity is less universal, with those works in which contextuality is a (or *the*) major consideration giving less attention to the historic particulars. Missing from all seven projects is an in-depth investigation of the relation of Christian faith to Judaism befitting our increasing awareness of the need for an antisupersessionist reinterpretation (and thus a locus on "covenant" or "Israelology," as in Hendrikus Berkhof's *Christian Faith*).

Conversation with the Community

Classical systematics is catholic, attending to the varied truth claimants within the church universal, working out positions in a knowledgeable rejection, modification or appropriation of their ideas. Each of our systematicians is also in dialogue with alternative readings of Christian doctrine, sometimes framing the choices in typology: Sölle's orthodox, liberal and liberation categories; Migliore's options on Scripture: biblicism, uncritical historicism, bourgeois privatism and detached aestheticism (Migliore, 43-46); Smart and Konstantine's options on authority and revelation: biblical assertions, the teachings of the community of believers or "anything conducive to the experience of the Transcendent" (Smart and Konstantine, 86, 99).

When the diversity within the contemporary Christian community is considered—taking as a small indication the variety of systematics earlier chronicled—one is struck by how restricted the conversation is in most of these works. Evans canvasses in helpful detail a range of twentieth-century African-American theologians on various topics but pays little attention throughout to classical thought or other current theological perspectives. The typologies cited above do not do justice to either the extent of current options or the variety within a given type, often falling prey to popular caricatures. Sölle's category of "orthodox," into which Jewett, Migliore and Peters presumably would fit, along with Barth and Pannenberg, silences the varied voices of "the other." So too, the frequent categorization and dismissal of evangelical theology by most of these authors as "fundamentalism" and "biblicism" show both a failure of conversational nerve and innocence of the phenomenon. (Ironically, and sadly to this ecumenical theologian, evangelical Jewett demonstrates a greater familiarity and willingness to dialogue with the range of current partisans than other purportedly ecumenical authors.) Another disappointment is the virtual absence of encounter with the *other* systematic/constructive theologies that have emerged in the past fifteen years.

Conclusions and Observation

Yes, systematic/constructive theology is very much with us. Yes, our sample suggests that these works tend to be in continuity with the defining characteristics of classical systematics, but unevenly so, some better at indwelling the tradition, engaging the culture or being topically inclusive than others, and most of them limited in catholicity of conversation. (Some not in our sample, notably Wolfhart Pannenberg's *Systematic Theology,* do excel on most counts.)

A concluding word on an unasked question: Why systematic/constructive theology now? Social location gives us one clue. Many of the authors of the seventy-odd projects teach in graduate schools of theology and are responsible for introductory courses or basic sequences. They have concluded that standard works of another day need to be supplemented or replaced by efforts in systematics *aggiornamento.* Another factor at work is sensitivity to the theological illiteracy of the current seminary generation, and thus the need to reintroduce the student to the tradition out of which they are expected to preach and teach, especially so when parishioners increasingly ask about it vis-à-vis today's competing ideologies. While all the current works speak to each of these concerns, the poles of "retrieval" and "reconstruction" suggest which of them—remembering or recontextualizing—is to the fore in a given venture.

The impetus to retrieve/remember and reconstruct/update correlates with the ecclesial and perspectival tendencies prominent in the current movement. The former expresses itself frequently in a "roots" phenomenon, the reentry of one's own heritage—Lutheran, Reformed, Roman Catholic, Baptist, African-American . . . The latter is associated with a heightened awareness of comradeship with those who share common experiences and frameworks. Both could be significant contributions to the theological enterprise, bringing neglected traditions or contexts to higher visibility. However, the danger of retribalizing the church and balkanizing theological discourse is also great, evidences of which are to be found in the limited range of interlocutors in the works considered.

For all the systematic shortfalls, the present quest for the comprehensive is a notable new development. And it brings with it a pledge to ferret out connections: with both the theological heritage and the historical context, among the individual doctrines, and among the diverse traditions and perspectives in the Christian community. These risks taken to see things whole, and to propose new ways to appropriate the web of Christian belief, can enrich all of our theological work.

Other Works Cited

Berkhof, Hendrikus. *Christian Faith: An Introduction to the Study of Faith*. Rev. ed. Grand Rapids, Mich.: Eerdmans, 1986.

Boice, James Montgomery. *Foundations of Christian Faith*. Rev. ed. Downers Grove, Ill.: InterVarsity Press, 1986.

Bloesch, Donald G. *Essentials of Evangelical Theology*. 2 vols. San Francisco: Harper & Row, 1978-1979.

——. *God the Almighty: Power, Wisdom, Holiness, Love*. Christian Foundations 3. Downers Grove, Ill.: InterVarsity Press, 1995.

——. *Holy Scripture: Revelation, Inspiration & Interpretation*. Christian Foundations 2. Downers Grove, Ill.: InterVarsity Press, 1994.

——. *Jesus Christ: Savior & Lord*. Christian Foundations 4. Downers Grove, Ill.: InterVarsity Press, 1997.

——. *A Theology of Word & Spirit: Authority & Method in Theology*. Christian

Foundations 1. Downers Grove, Ill.: InterVarsity Press, 1992.

Borowitz, Eugene B. *Renewing the Covenant: A Theology for the Postmodern Jew*. Philadelphia: Jewish Publication Society, 1991.

Braaten, Carl E., and Robert W. Jenson, eds. *Christian Dogmatics*. 2 vols. Philadelphia: Fortress, 1984.

Cauthen, Kenneth. *Systematic Theology: A Modern Protestant Approach*. Lewistown, N.Y.: Edwin Mellen Press, 1986.

Chopp, Rebecca S., and Mark Lewis Taylor, eds. *Reconstructing Christian Theology*. Minneapolis: Fortress, 1994.

Cone, James. *A Black Theology of Liberation*. Philadelphia: J. B. Lippincott, 1970.

Conyers, A. J. *A Basic Christian Theology*. Nashville: Broadman & Holman, 1995.

Dunning, H. Ray. *Grace, Faith and Holiness: A Wesleyan Systematic Theology*. Kansas City, Mo.: Beacon Hill, 1988.

Erickson, Millard J. *Christian Theology*. 3 vols. Grand Rapids, Mich.: Baker Book House, 1983-1985.

Fackre, Gabriel. *The Christian Story*. Vol. 1, *A Narrative Intepretation of Christian Doctrine*. 2nd rev. ed. Grand Rapids, Mich.: Eerdmans, 1996.

――――. *The Christian Story*. Vol. 2, *Authority: Scripture in the Church for the World*. Grand Rapids, Mich.: Eerdmans, 1987.

Finger, Thomas N. *Christian Theology: An Eschatological Approach*. 2 vols. Scottdale, Penn.: Herald, 1987-1989.

Garrett, James Leo. *Systematic Theology: Biblical, Historical and Evangelical*. 2 vols. Grand Rapids, Mich.: Eerdmans, 1990-1995.

Gilkey, Langdon. *Message and Existence: An Introduction to Christian Theology*. New York: Seabury Press, 1979.

Grenz, Stanley J. *Theology for the Community of God*. Nashville: Broadman & Holman, 1994.

Grudem, Wayne A. *Systematic Theology: An Introduction to Biblical Doctrine*. Grand Rapids, Mich.: Zondervan, 1994.

Gutiérrez, Gustavo. *A Theology of Liberation: History, Politics and Salvation*. Translated and edited by Sister Caridad Inda and John Eagleson. Maryknoll, N.Y.: Orbis Books, 1973, 1988.

Hall, Douglas John. *Confessing the Faith: Christian Theology in a North American Context*. Minneapolis: Fortress, 1997.

――――. *Professing the Faith: Christian Theology in a North American Context*. Minneapolis: Fortress, 1993.

――――. *Thinking the Faith: Christian Theology in a North American Context*. Minneapolis: Augsburg, 1989.

Hanson, A. T., and R. P. C. Hanson. *Reasonable Belief: A Survey of the Christian Faith*. Oxford: Oxford University Press, 1980.

Henry, Carl F. H. *God, Revelation and Authority*. 6 vols. Waco, Tex.: Word, 1976-1983.

Herzog, Frederick. *God-Walk: Liberation Shaping Dogmatics.* Maryknoll, N.Y.: Orbis Books, 1988.

Hodgson, Peter. *Winds of the Spirit: A Constructive Christian Theology.* Louisville, Ky.: Westminster John Knox Press, 1994.

Hodgson, Peter C., and Robert H. King, eds. *Christian Theology: An Introduction to Its Traditions and Tasks.* Rev. ed. Philadelphia: Fortress, 1994.

Jenson, Robert. *Systematic Theology.* 2 vols. New York: Oxford University Press, 1997-1998.

Jewett, Paul K., with Marguerite Shuster. *God, Creation and Revelation: A Neo-evangelical Theology.* Grand Rapids, Mich.: Eerdmans, 1991.

———. *Who We Are: Our Dignity as Human: A Neo-evangelical Theology.* Grand Rapids, Mich.: Eerdmans, 1996.

Johnson, Alan F., and Robert E. Webber. *What Christians Believe: A Biblical and Historical Summary.* Grand Rapids, Mich.: Zondervan/Academie Books, 1989.

Kaufman, Gordon. *In Face of Mystery: A Constructive Theology.* Cambridge, Mass.: Harvard University Press, 1993.

Leith, John H. *Basic Christian Doctrine.* Louisville, Ky.: Westminster John Knox Press, 1993.

Lewis, Gordon R., and Bruce A. Demarest. *Integrative Theology.* 3 vols. Grand Rapids, Mich.: Zondervan/Academie Books, 1987-1994.

Lightner, Robert. *Evangelical Theology: A Survey and Review.* Grand Rapids, Mich.: Baker Book House, 1986.

Lochman, Jan. *The Faith We Confess: An Ecumenical Dogmatics.* Translated by David Lewis. Philadelphia: Fortress, 1984.

McBrien, Richard P. *Catholicism.* Rev. ed. San Francisco: HarperSanFrancisco, 1994.

McClendon, James William. *Systematic Theology.* 2 vols. Nashville: Abingdon, 1986-1994.

McGrath, Alister E. *Christian Theology: An Introduction.* Oxford: Blackwell, 1994.

Menzies, William W. *Bible Doctrines: A Pentecostal Perspective.* Revised and expanded by Stanley M. Horton. Springfield, Mo.: Logian, 1993.

Moltmann, Jürgen. *The Coming of God: Christian Eschatology.* Translated by Margaret Kohl. Minneapolis: Fortress, 1996.

———. *God in Creation: A New Theology of Creation and the Spirit of God.* Translated by Margaret Kohl. San Francisco: Harper & Row, 1985.

———. *The Spirit of Life: A Universal Affirmation.* Translated by Margaret Kohl. London: SCM Press, 1992.

———. *The Trinity and the Kingdom: The Doctrine of God.* Translated by Margaret Kohl. San Francisco: Harper & Row, 1981.

———. *The Way of Jesus Christ: Christology in Messianic Dimensions.* Translated by Margaret Kohl. San Francisco: HarperSanFrancisco, 1990.

Moody, Dale. *The Word of Truth.* Grand Rapids, Mich.: Eerdmans, 1981.

Morse, Christopher. *Not Every Spirit: A Dogmatics of Christian Disbelief.* Valley Forge, Penn.: Trinity Press International, 1994.

Oden, Thomas. *Systematic Theology.* 3 vols. San Francisco: Harper & Row/HarperSanFrancisco, 1987-1992.

Pannenberg, Wolfhart. *Systematic Theology.* 3 vols. Translated by Geoffrey W. Bromiley. Grand Rapids, Mich.: Eerdmans, 1991-1998.

Pomazansky, Michael. *Orthodox Dogmatic Theology: A Concise Exposition.* Translated by Seraphim Rose. Platina, Calif.: Saint Herman of Alaska Brotherhood, 1984.

Rice, Richard. *The Reign of God: An Introduction to Christian Theology from a Seventh-Day Adventist Perspective.* Berrian Springs, Mich.: Andrews University Press, 1985.

Suchocki, Marjorie Hewitt. *God, Christ, Church.* New York: Crossroad, 1982.

Schwarz, Hans. *Responsible Faith: Christian Theology in the Light of 20th-Century Questions.* Minneapolis: Augsburg, 1986.

Schüssler Fiorenza, Francis, and John Galvin, eds. *Systematic Theology: Roman Catholic Perspectives.* 2 vols. Minneapolis: Fortress, 1991.

Spykman, Gordon. *Reformational Theology: A New Paradigm for Doing Dogmatics.* Grand Rapids, Mich.: Eerdmans, 1992.

Thielicke, Helmut. *The Evangelical Faith.* 3 vols. Translated and edited by Geoffrey W. Bromiley. Grand Rapids, Mich.: Eerdmans, 1974-1982.

Thistlethwaite, Susan Brooks, and Mary Potter Engel, eds. *Lift Every Voice: Constructing Christian Theologies from the Underside.* San Francisco: Harper & Row, 1990.

van Beeck, Frans Jozef, S.J. *God Encountered: A Contemporary Catholic Systematic Theology.* Vol. 1, *Understanding the Christian Faith.* 2nd rev. ed. Collegeville, Minn.: Liturgical Press, 1993.

———. *God Encountered: A Contemporary Catholic Systematic Theology.* Vol. 2, part 1, *The Revelation of the Glory.* San Francisco: Harper & Row, 1989.

van Buren, Paul M. *A Theology of the Jewish Christian Reality.* Vol. 1, *Discerning the Way.* New York: Seabury Press, 1980.

———. *A Theology of the Jewish Christian Reality.* Vol. 2, *A Christian Theology of the People Israel.* New York: Seabury Press, 1983.

———. *A Theology of the Jewish Christian Reality.* Vol. 3, *Christ in Context.* San Francisco: Harper & Row, 1987.

Wainwright, Geoffrey. *Doxology.* New York: Oxford University Press, 1980.

Weber, Otto. *Foundations of Dogmatics.* 2 vols. Translated by Darrel L. Guder. Grand Rapids, Mich.: Eerdmans, 1982-1983.

Williams, J. Rodman. *Renewal Theology.* 3 vols. Grand Rapids, Mich.: Zondervan/Academie Books, 1988-1992.

8

An Altar Call
for Evangelicals†

BORN-AGAIN CHRISTIANS ON THE RECEIVING END OF A CALL TO REPENTANCE? Yes, if a leading evangelical scholar has his way. In a groundbreaking new book, Gordon-Conwell theologian David Wells charges that there is "no place for truth" in the ranks of many of the popular preachers and teachers, journals, bookstores, media ventures and megachurches of today's fast-growing evangelicalism. The reason? Like the earlier twentieth-century modernists whose eagerness to be relevant emptied the faith of its substance, evangelicalism has capitulated to the processes and premises of our late twentieth-century culture.

Wells grounds his case in a detailed analysis of the centrifugal forces of modernization—urbanization, specialization, the interlocking systems of market, media, government, education (all in transnational configurations)—that shape our culture's assumptions and have taken evangelicalism hostage. "Modernity" is the set of values—secular, privatized, pluralist, relativist—associated with modernization. (The literature of "postmodernity" is discussed as a development within modernity.) The American psyche and character adapted to this technosocial

†This review of David F. Wells, *No Place for Truth* (Grand Rapids, Mich.: Eerdmans, 1993), was first published in *The Christian Century* 110 (November 17-24, 1994): 1167-69.

environment is self-absorbed, as evidenced in its current therapeutic fads and fancies. Succumbing to narcissism, our society is awash in both individualism and conformity, focused on self-fulfillment rather than truth, and thus drifting into moral normlessness and anomie.

Wells's analysis draws selectively on a company of present-day critics and students of modern culture—Christopher Lasch, Robert Bellah, Peter Berger, Robert Wuthnow, Alasdair MacIntyre and John Patrick Donnelly among others—and on the social commentary of earlier decades—David Riesman, Philip Rieff, Robert Nisbet, Alvin Toffler, Daniel Boorstin, Jacques Ellul, Michael Harrington and Ann Douglas. The stage is set for the correlation of sociological diagnosis with theological jeremiad in an opening chapter on the effects over time of modernization cum modernity on the Boston suburb of Wenham, with the marginalization and cultural accommodation of its formerly central church and faith. (The building of the Puritan congregation on the green, now First Congregational Church, UCC Wenham, is on the cover of the book.)

Wells argues that evangelical faith, once rooted in "historic Protestant orthodoxy," was countercultural and cognitively dissident. Now its "breathless new followers" with their "paper-thin piety" are simply a religious version of today's popular "self movement," preoccupied not with the costly demands of truth but with personal enrichments, and thus captive to "Our Time." Apparent everywhere are "vacuous worship," preaching prodigal with the "nostrums of the therapeutic age" (101) where "the audience [not the holy God] is sovereign" (207), a "strident pragmatism" (95) of management techniques, a pollster-oriented piety, and a glossy materialism in its public appearances and strategies. Low points are reached in the "health and wealth gospel" of its less inhibited entrepreneurs and in a megachurch exhibitionism, with its "skydivers dropping in during a sermon . . . and prayer groups outfitting themselves in combat fatigues" (174).

While "Christian beliefs have been mostly retained," they are "not allowed to encumber the search for new forms of spirituality, technique and community" (110). No wonder, Wells says, that the historic moral agenda of evangelicalism has had no public effect on a country in which a third of the population identifies itself as "born-again."

In contrast to fundamentalist diatribes against "secular humanism," Wells is here targeting a "secular evangelicalism" (79). In fact, he believes that its ranks include many of the shrillest foes of secularism, whose protests may have more to do with a "culture war . . . [and] the desire to retain the old power" (111) than with theological integrity. He also faults the sloganeers of secular humanism for their failure to discern the sociological substructure of the ideas they attack.

When evangelicals seek "health and success rather than truth" (294), the author contends that "theology" is the loser. He also states the case in reverse, showing that the evangelical abandonment of theology results in evangelicalism's capitulation to Our Time.

What is "theology" in Wells's view? Not, of course, the generalized academic inquiries about things religious, or the Our Time doctrine of the liberal theological establishment. Rather, theology, "driven by a passion for truth" (12), is (1) the confessional core of a biblical orthodoxy, (2) comprehensive and coherent reflection thereupon in relation to cultural issues and idiom, and (3) a "wisdom" expressed in virtues that live out this apostolic confession and reflection. Theology so conceived, with its purpose the nurture of the people of God, once stood at the center of evangelical faith, and still belongs there. But now "an antitheological mood has gripped the evangelical world" (98), manifest in the preaching and teaching of evangelical churches, its literature, radio and television programs—directions charted in the headquarters of evangelical denominations and in too much of the curriculum, ethos and student body of evangelical seminaries.

A thirty-year period in the publication of *Christianity Today*—from 1959 to 1989—is used as a case study in retreat from theological substance to market-oriented news and topical personal and therapeutic subjects. Another study, this time of articles in the 1980-1988 period of the widely read evangelical clergy journal *Leadership,* reveals that "less than 1 percent of the material made any clear reference to Scripture, still less to any idea that is theological" (114). For Wells, one of the more blatant examples of "riding the streams of modernity" is the self-esteem less-sin-and-substance gospel of Robert Schuller, a "biting parody of American self-absorption" (175).

While we must wait for two planned sequel volumes (since published as *God in the Wasteland* and *Losing our Virtue*) for the details of Wells's proposals for an evangelical turnaround, indicators are here discernible. One of them is the judgment that cultural disarray and evangelical fumbling may themselves be a "strange ground of hope, . . . [for] God . . . often pulls down and plucks up" (91) before reformation and rebuilding. Another is a challenge to anthropocentrism ("the small and tawdry interest of the self in itself" 185) by an evangelical theocentrism with its "vision of humanity corrupted by sin being released to stand before God in all his glory and converse with him, gripped by the magnificent certainty of his truth" (185). Such a vision is of a piece with a strong form of narrative theology (revealed propositions interpreting divine deeds, not subjectivist stories or cultural-linguistic community tales) as that is derived from an inerrant (though not dictationally oracular) Scripture. Its stewards will be theologian-pastors willing to be "sacred fools" who tell the embarrassing truth to church and culture.

The specifics of his proposals aside, Wells is deploying within his own community an evangelical hermeneutic of suspicion. As such, he functions as a "critic-in-residence," a social role Donald Michaels holds to be necessary for the viability of any institution or movement.

Whatever Happened to Ecumenical Theology?

Let mainliners tempted to chortle over the exposure of evangelicalism's flaws first consider their own clay feet. These are parlous days for theological centering in ecumenical circles too. Schuller is popular in mainline as well as evangelical "markets." Establishment church bureaucracies show as little interest in theological substance as their evangelical counterparts. Consumer studies and market inducements are *de rigueur* in mainline seminary programs and policies. The literature of therapy and management dominates our conference book tables as well as the shelves of Christian bookstores. Cultural orthodoxies—from the magisterium of both the *New York Times* and the checkout counter tabloids—show up regularly in our preaching and teaching.

Wells makes reference to mainline acculturation along the edges of his critique of evangelicalism, tracing its beginnings to the earlier "Liberal" quest for relevance with its slogan "not doctrine but life," in both Protestantism and Catholic modernism. He also remarks upon today's capitulations of mainline/ecumenical churches and theology (with acknowledgment of a brief interruption by Barth's protests), citing such things as a professionalized clergy's quest for social status with suspect

D.Min. degrees, and the collapse of theological vertebrae in its guild and in university religious studies programs. Wells distinguishes the two versions of cultural captivity as the difference between the liberal accession to "high culture" and evangelical enticement by "low culture," along with the former's active accommodationist intentions compared to the latter's passive susceptibilities.

What might go on in a give-and-take between mainline and evangelical critics-in-residence? For one, a mutual recognition of restiveness in both camps. Indeed, Wells acknowledges some signs of internal scrutiny and calls for reorientation in ecumenical circles. He also draws upon them for his own analysis: the earlier sober self-examinations of Van Harvey, Edward Farley, Langdon Gilkey and Sidney Mead, and the more recent pleas from various quarters for "resident aliens," faithfulness to the biblical narrative, and retrieval of the classical loci in systematic theology. Wells knows, too, that he has allies in evangelical discontent, alluding as he does to the works of Os Guinness, James Davison Hunter, Mark Noll, George Marsden, Nathan Hatch, Joel Carpenter and Alister McGrath. And there is much more evidence of critics-in-residence in both constituencies than that cited: pastors recentering in lectionary study and theological table-talk groups, laity relearning their theological ABCs, confessional and evangelical catholic reclamations in denominational life, the "gospel and culture" efforts of Lesslie Newbigin and friends, the serious theological work done in bilateral dialogues and in ecumenical forums like the BEM and the Apostolic Faith studies of the World Council of Churches, signs of theological recentering in mainline seminaries—including the upgrading of D.Min. degrees—some publishing houses risking theological solidities in a market of "paper-thin piety," and some directional reconsiderations in mainline journals.

Kindred minds need to become acquainted with one another. For ecumenicals that means less ignorance and caricature of evangelicals. This work is must reading for them, shattering many stereotypes with its mastery of the literature of cultural criticism, its willingness to admit the serious limitations of its own tradition, and the literary grace with which its case is made. Furthermore, by focusing on evangelical self-examination, it invites a parallel ecumenical soul-searching that the currently popular mainline church-bashing can never induce.

In this exchange, ecumenicals will have admonitions as well as affirmations for evangelicals. (The formulation "mutual affirmation and admonition" comes from the North American Lutheran-Reformed document *Our Common Calling.*) Because they have been there before, both tempted by the allurements of culture and seeking to wrench loose therefrom, they know a little about the occupational hazards of resident alienry and criticism-in-residence. One of those pitfalls is self-righteous fury: "Thank God, I am not as others!" So the question comes: Is there a "mea culpa" by the critic along with the indictment? Ecumenicals, as heirs to the central tradition of the church, do have a confession of sin in their liturgies to remind them ever and again of their continuing complicity in the Fall. Such is not common practice for evangelicalism, the boundaries of which are established by the experience of new birth, with calls to confession issued to those outside. With that goes the temptation to define the world too simplistically as a contest between "us and them," the armies of light and night—even when excommunicating their own. But authentic prophecy is as penitent as it is polemical, acknowledging the temptations to theological hauteur, and also the ambiguities and ironies of its own position.

Ecumenicals will also have admonitions about the meaning of theology, reminding evangelicals of the implications of a feature of the historic faith in which they both are rooted: the covenant with Noah. In the language of Wells's Reformed tradition, the promise of a "common grace" that sustains the world after the Fall assures enough small light in all creation to keep the story going forward, and thus makes Christians attentive to truth wherever found. So those of secular stripe who rub our conscience raw with their charges of injustice, who press upon us the struggle for peace or ecological sanity, who bring critical tools to the study of the human underside of Scripture, who force us to face the realities of pluralism, may well be Assyrian rods God uses to chasten our insularities. Why not such common grace even among the Nebuchadnezzars of a dangerous modernity? While the therapeutic idols of the day need to be brought down, healing wherever it happens cannot be scorned by those who sing "There is a balm in Gilead."

Extrabiblical "human experience" can never occupy the center of theological authority. Its drift to that location has been the ecumenical Achilles heel to which both the Barths and the Wellses have every right to point. Nevertheless, God's universal grace of preservation through the voice of the "other" regularly opens our eyes to things in the gospel we had missed and makes us face issues we would rather avoid. Indeed, a later Barth acknowledged something of that (IV/3/1) in his talk of God's worldly "free communications" and "parables of the kingdom." A christologically accountable doctrine of "general revelation" (affirmed by Wells as part of the evangelical tradition) can do the same. In all this we remember as well that a romanticism of the past is no solution for mesmerism with the present; Their Time has as many seductions as Our Time.

And again, some ecumenical counsel on the theology of "powers and principalities," one not so different from that of the self-identified "justice and peace evangelicals": Remember the Roxburys as well as the Wenhams . . . and what goes on, or doesn't go on, in the latter that impacts the former. With the social-order sensibilities of his Reformed heritage, Wells does speak about how systems affect persons and even casts a critical eye on our market economy. But there is no clear theological mandate to engage the sociopolitical powers and principalities comparable to the prophetic challenge to cultural captivity. While ecumenical theology and churches have their own activist temptations, evangelical theology and churches have their quietist ones.

Almost three decades have passed since Harvey Cox celebrated the dynamisms of "the secular city" and called for a church attuned to its rhythms and at home in its environs. Taking the same greater Boston as paradigmatic, Wells draws a much more somber picture of cosmopolitan America and laments his own tradition's Babylonian captivity. Roxbury mutings apart, and hindsight considered, Wells has the better part of the argument. To move on from here means self-critical evangelicals and ecumenicals asking: Can we make common cause in a new realism about the pitfalls of modernity? In the recovery of theological focus? In the reinterpretation of ancient faith and not the repristination of ancient formulas? In affirming and admonishing one another?

All this may be too much to hope for in our tribalist era. Yet if it is true that "this world with devils filled may threaten to undo us," then the time has come for would-be reformers to come together for what Luther called "mutual conversation and consolation," and what must added to that: "mutual correction."

9

Whither Evangelicalism?[†]

A RECENT WHEATON COLLEGE CONFERENCE EXPLORED THE POSSIBLE CON-
vergences between "evangelicals and postliberals."[1] Last year a Messiah College consultation brought together "evangelicals and
ecumenicals" in the research project Re-forming the Center. Concur-
rently, alliances are urged between "evangelicals and Catholics."
What then of evangelicals "on the road to Canterbury, Constanti-
nople, Rome"? And the standard-brand evangelicals who gather in
the hundreds of thousands in Promise Keeper stadiums, the millions
in the Christian Coalition and the billion who tune in to a worldwide
Billy Graham telecast? Which way the evangelical empire? And just
what is an "evangelical" anyway?

The word *evangelical* in original Reformation context is associated
with its "formal principle" of biblical authority and its "material
principle" of justification by faith.[2] Evangelicalism today is the inten-
sification and interiorization of each: a devotional use of Scripture

[†]This essay was originally published in *Pro Ecclesia* 6 (Winter 1997): 12-15.

with a hermeneutic of either inerrancy or infallibility, and a "born-again" experience of justification with outcomes in evangelistic zeal, personal piety and morality. For all that, evangelicalism is a very diverse movement, depending on what facet is accented. An evangelical fundamentalism draws the line in the sand at inerrancy, and a political fundamentalism transposes the either-or of the new birth experience into an us-and-them mindset in the public arena. "Old evangelicals" focus on evangelism, "new evangelicals" on apologetics, "ecumenical evangelicals" on movement out of stereotypes. And then there are the new "postevangelicals," and more.

"Evangelical catholics" in the tradition of *Pro Ecclesia* should attend carefully to the diversity and new directions in contemporary evangelicalism, especially so in this time of church struggle in mainline denominations. Where basic doctrine is at stake, ecumenical evangelicals and evangelical catholics will find themselves walking together. It happens in the current "center" and neoconfessional movements, whether organized as in the UCC's "Confessing Christ" constituency or in the tacit partnerships of the more diffuse centrist atmosphere described in Jack Rogers's *Claiming the Center*. Wherever the authority of Scripture, the ecumenical creeds and Reformation confessions, and classical teaching on the Trinity and the person and work of Christ have been rejected or marginalized by current ideologies, ecumenically open evangelicals will keep company with evangelical catholic kin. The Re-imagining Conference and its sequel events, the move to alter the universal trinitarian formula, the construal of one form of inclusive language as normative in hymnody and liturgy (there are at least eleven varieties),[3] the introduction of religious relativisms into denominational literature, the courting of Jesus Seminar figures and ideas—all these invite common concern and witness.

While unabashedly polemical on issues of basic Christian identity, the same wing of evangelicalism lately has been sounding a strong note of self-criticism. Under attack by major evangelical theologians are the narcissisms, self-help ideologies, experientialisms and cultural accommodations of evangelical megachurches, radio and television personalities, and Christian bookstore bestsellers. The jeremiads of David Wells, Alister McGrath, Os Guinness and Richard Lints, among others, call for the return of evangelicals to biblical, doctrinal and catechetical solidities, modeling the same in their own writings. All this is reminiscent of the nineteenth-century evangelical catholic critique of pietist excesses and the call for liturgical reform and catechetical faithfulness, as in the Mercersburg theologians' (Nevin and Schaff) response to the "anxious bench" and frontier revivalism.

Of particular note in the doctrinal retrieval of evangelicalism is the work of its systematic theologians. They were among the first in the 1970s to attempt the rehabilitation of discipline with full-scale efforts in visiting the classical loci. They are now in the front ranks of those writing major works in the field, among them Donald Bloesch, Millard Erickson, Alister McGrath, Thomas Oden, Stanley Grenz, Gordon Lewis and Bruce Demarest, Paul Jewett, Leo Garrett Jr., Robert Lightner, William Rodman, James Montgomery Boice, Richard Rice and A. J. Conyers. These evangelical theologians are all male and white, a fact prompting yet further evangelical soul-searching. However, women and ethnic evangelical theologians are making their voices heard in the pages of *Daughters of Sarah,* a volume like *The Goddess Revival* (by Aida Besançon Spencer, Donna F. G. Hailson, Catherine Clark Kroeger), and in the works of Willie Jennings, Orlando Costas, Samuel Solivan and Eldine Villafane.

Evangelical self-criticism includes the acknowledged absence of an articulate Christ-culture voice. So Mark Noll's brilliant indictment in *The Scandal of the Evangelical Mind.* But things are changing here too. The journal *Books and Culture* specializes in learned and lively evangelical commentary on science, literature and the arts, on the ideas and institutions of modernity and postmodernity. An evangelical catholicity of mind as well as doctrine cannot help but be instructed and edified by this fare.

Not all in evangelicalism is ecumenical polemics and self-critical irenics. Some polemics is misfired and schismatic, and some irenics is soft-headed and accommodationist. For example, in the first case, ultra-evangelicals often fix on cultural rather than theological issues. Earlier, Carl McIntire gave pride of place in his assaults to fluoridation and the United Nations. Today homosexuality and abortion come front and center. What are arguably either second-rank ethical issues or disputed questions somewhat short of a "mind of the church" catholic are raised to church-dividing, and even Christ-defining, status. Thus the culture wars, ironically, set the agenda for a purportedly gospel-oriented faith. Self-styled "biblical renewal" movements of conservative evangelicals have too often fallen prey to these cultural seductions, failing to address the underlying theological issues. Acceding to the culture-war judgments on where lines are to be drawn is also regularly accompanied by a Manichaean us-and-them mentality, one fueled by the sharp before-and-after disjunctions of the new birth experience. Here an evangelical catholic admonition is in order, having to do with the *simul iustus et peccator* of the Christian life with its Niebuhrian transposition to culture matters.

The hard-edged schismatic tendency of the evangelical right is matched by the wooly-minded irenics of the evangelical left. It is painful to this evangelical catholic to sit through an AAR meeting listening to evangelical commendation of the pluralism of Paul Knitter, while ecumenical Mark Heim minces no words in his demolition of the same (as in his *Salvations*). Troubling also to see arguments for "the openness of God" and "unbounded love: good news for the twenty-first century" (recent book titles of Clark Pinnock, Robert Brow et al.) that appear to step on all the mines unearthed by the Barths, Bonhoeffers and Niebuhrs of the twentieth century. Unnerving as well, at the Wheaton and Messiah conferences mentioned earlier, to hear some evangelicals repudiate their heritage of biblical authority and doctrinal orthodoxy along with the rightly rejected oppressive forms that housed them. Ecumenicals have business to do with evangelicals, a matter often of reading them the minutes of the last meeting.

Whither evangelicalism? Given the diversity, better the more specific question of "whither evangelical catholic and ecumenical evangelical relations?" The possibilities are there, right now, for a moment of mutual conversation and consolation: mutual conversation about perils to a common classical Christianity, and mutual consolation of comrades in a church struggle for theological integrity. There is even the possibility of mutual edification. Linked together, evangelical catholics can learn something as well as give something, appreciating more the disciplines of personal piety, a daily in-depth encounter with Scripture, and the importance of the evangelism mandate. For both, this is a "whither" worth walking together.

10

A New Ecumenism[†]
Mutual Affirmation & Admonition

ECUMENICAL DIRECTIONS WERE CHARTED IN THE SUMMER OF 1997 THAT could "begin a dramatic new chapter in the near five-century history of the Reformation." So said Gunther Gassmann, former director of the WCC's Faith and Order Commission about proposals before the Evangelical Lutheran Church in America (*Dialog*, Spring 1996, p. 139) before the vote. The result? A vote to approve "full communion" with three Reformed churches (the Presbyterian Church, U.S.A., the Reformed Church in America and the United Church of Christ), the mutual lifting of sixteenth-century Lutheran-Roman Catholic condemnations, and the near-approval of a "concordat" with the Episcopal Church—up for probable acceptance in 1999 after a rewrite.

Why, from this Reformed participant's viewpoint, are these decisions and directions so important? A formula put forward in the Lutheran-Reformed document *A Common Calling* sheds light on a

[†]This essay was first published as "What the Lutherans and the Reformed Can Learn from One Another," *The Christian Century* 114 (June 4-11, 1997): 558-61. It received the first-place award for "Topic of the Year: Ecumenism" from the Associated Church Press.

fresh premise argued in detail in this proposal and presupposed in the others: "mutual affirmation *and* mutual admonition." *Mutual affirmation* means sufficient commonality to take the stipulated steps forward. *Mutual admonition* means acknowledgment of the positive import of historic differences. Can the differences, until now the cause of separation, be viewed in a new ecumenical context as legitimate varying perspectives on the commonalities and thus not church-dividing? And more, are they needed *emphases*, charisms in the church catholic, brought to the fore by historical circumstance? And possibly even more: can these historic differences be complementary to, and even *corrective* of, one another?

Mutual affirmation is standard in ecumenical negotiations, and is integral also to the Lutheran-Reformed proposal: "If you hold to these essentials, we can take a step toward you." Mutual admonition goes further, requiring the willingness of each to affirm the *differences* as well as the similarities, thus forswearing inordinate claims that have said to the other, "I have no need of you" (1 Cor 12:21). While we may be right in what we affirm, we may be wrong in what we deny or ignore. Thus, if one's own Corinthian charism does not, in principle, preclude the other, the time has come to cease denying or ignoring it. *By the same token,* admonition is the warning to the other that the exclusion of one's own gift is a wound in the body of Christ and an impoverishment of the gospel. The tough-mindedness in this proposal prompts the ecumenist Harding Myer to say that "there is definitely something new about it. This 'new' element is that now a clearly *positive function* is being attributed to the differences, the function of mutual admonition, or mutual correction, of being 'no-trespassing signs'" (*Ecumenical Trends,* September 1994, pp. 116-17).

Solidarity and Sovereignty

Historic Lutheran and Reformed disputes are a showcase of what it would mean to move to these mutualities. Lutheran-Reformed diversity is manifest in matters that run from sacramental theology, worship practice, confessional subscription and understandings of grace to concepts of social witness and personal piety. One way to sum up the differences is by some historic fighting-words: the Lutheran *finitum capax infiniti* vs. the Reformed *finitum non capax infiniti* (the finite is capable . . . is not capable . . . of receiving the infinite). Put otherwise, Lutheran stewardship of the Reformation's "justification by faith" has accented its communication through Christ's continuing *solidarity with us* in ecclesial tangibilities. The Reformed interpretation of the same emphasizes justification under Christ's continuing *sovereignty over us* in both church and world.

Some early Bonhoeffer-Barth commentary brings to the surface just this distinction. Identifying his own Lutheran perspective with the *capax* accent, Bonhoeffer contrasts Barth's stress on God's "freedom on the far side of us" with his own view of God in Christ as "haveable, graspable within his Word within the Church" (*Act and Being,* p. 91). Barth, on the other hand, in a discussion of confessions, asserts the Reformed *non capax,* contending that historic texts, while a resource for interpreting Scripture, are accountable to a sovereignty beyond them and thus reformable, providing therefore for "*no* Augsburg Confession . . . *no* Formula of Concord . . . which might later, like the Lutheran, come to possess the odor of sanctity" (*The Word of God and the Word of Man,* p. 231).

The difference between Lutheran solidarity and Reformed sovereignty can be tracked in several arenas.

1. Debates on the Eucharist, with the Lutheran insistence on the ubiquity of Christ's human nature warranting the body and blood "in, with and under" the elements, in contrast to the Reformed insistence on participation in the body and blood by ascent through the power of the Spirit to the divine-human Person at the right hand of God "above" the elements. Mutual admonition means that Lutherans have a right to worry about Reformed sovereignty leading to the dissolution of the eucharistic Presence, and the Reformed have a right to be concerned about the Lutheran "haveability" domesticating the Presence. The differences are real, are necessary testimonies to an aspect of eucharistic teaching, and are warnings about the other's reductionist temptations.

2. The function of confessions earlier noted, with the Lutheran adherence to an unalterable sixteenth-century corpus of writings and the Reformed committed to updating and revising its doctrinal lore. The former stewards the Reformation doctrinal landmarks as signs of the divine faithfulness with and in the historic church and is

rightly wary of the temptation to accommodate the gospel to every new cultural twist and turn. The latter stewards the *semper refor-manda* in which the divine sovereignty calls for the recontextualization of the ancient faith and is rightly wary of the captivity of the gospel to formulations of the past.

3. The social mission of the church in which the Lutheran tradition has emphasized the doctrine of vocation, Christ's solidarity with the church expressing itself in its laity being "Christ to the neighbor" *within* the structures of society, while the Reformed tradition has emphasized Christ's sovereignty *over* both church and society calling the church, qua church, to shape society to the glory of God in obedience to Christ's regency in the secular realm. Lutherans remind the Reformed churches of their temptation to reduce mission to social action, to invite theocracy and/or to accede to current ideologies of the political left or right. The Reformed remind Lutherans of the temptations of quietism, of uncritical acceptance of the status quo as "orders of creation," and of a retreat from the ecclesial call to venture systemic change.

There are many other points of Lutheran-Reformed disagreement that reflect the solidarity/sovereignty distinctions, such as the historic Reformed stress in soteriology on the doctrine of "election" in contrast to the Lutheran accent on the appropriation of salvation in personal faith and its communication through the sacramental means of grace; in Christology, the Reformed temptation of Nestorianism and the Lutheran temptation of Monophysitism; in worship patterns, the respective emphases on pulpit and altar. And so on.

Simultaneity and Sanctification

Mutual corrigibility and complementarity could also address another long-standing Lutheran-Reformed difference, again captured in historic Latin battle cries: the Lutheran *simul iustus et peccator* (at the same time righteous and sinner) and the Reformed *sanctificatio* (not only the declaration of an alien righteousness but a becoming holy as both possibility and imperative). Lutherans stress the persistence of sin in the life of the redeemed, and the Reformed accent the growth in grace and the call to obedience of the believer through the "third use of the law." Lutherans, while also speaking of sanctification, are wary of a preoccupation with it that invites pretensions to perfectionism or falls prey to a righteousness based on works. Reformed, also sober about persisting sin, are concerned about a one-note stress on it that obscures a grace that both makes for and calls for holiness in the Christian life and society.

This particular difference provides an occasion for illustrating how varying Lutheran-Reformed perspectives can come together in a mutually fructifying way. No such actual convergence is required by an admonitory ecumenical proposal, only the acknowledgment of the legitimate witness of the other and an invitation to learning from the other by walking together. However, the theology of Reinhold Niebuhr, shaped as it was by both these traditions in his early years in the Evangelical Synod of North America, evidences the copresence of Lutheran simultaneity and Reformed sanctification. His Gifford lecture conjunction of justifying grace as "mercy toward us" and sanctifying grace as "power in us" is background to an overall theology of history that transposes these accents from the personal Christian life to the public arena.

Niebuhr appropriates the Reformed mandate to strive for change and its hope for genuine advance, sanctification translated into the social struggle and the "infinite possibilities" of history, a commitment he finds most clearly in a later Calvinism. Yet at the same time he deploys the Lutheran sobriety about the corruptibility of every historical advance, made more seductive just when it appears more virtuous, and when corrupted, more consequential in its devastating effects. Allied with this partnership of vision and realism is his version of the Lutheran two-kingdom theory that distinguishes between achievable goals in a fallen world and the eschatological norm of *agapē*. But at the same time he holds the modest possibilities of the kingdom of the left hand also to be accountable to the regnant Christ, the Reformed standard of a radical love that never lets us rest comfortable with society's givens.

In sovereignty/solidarity matters, Niebuhr's deficient doctrine of the church has little Lutheran sacramentality, while the Reformed doctrine of sovereignty functions actively in his ethics. Yet his memorable prayer captures something of the dialectic with "the courage to change" reflecting Reformed imperatives and possibilities and "the serenity to accept" reminiscent of Lutheran assurances about grace in the givens. Niebuhr's own example of convergence, while utopian in current church negotiations, can serve as a goad in the latter toward what he called elsewhere an "impossible possibility."

Getting Down to Cases

Historic significance, the commendations of ecumenical observers and the existence of a complementarity model, to the contrary notwithstanding, sharp questions are raised in some quarters about the Lutheran-Reformed proposal. Three issues recur, all having to do with the risks of a mutuality of affirmation and admonition.

1. Are the affirmations of common belief in the texts and traditions of all the partners *in fact* espoused by the congregations and clergy of the participating churches? My own denomination, the United Church of Christ, is regularly instanced with anecdotal evidence as theologically incoherent.

The question is a fair one. Full communion in bilateral ecumenics—or the comparable "covenant communion" in multilaterals like the nine-denomination *Consultation on Church Union*—requires a theological consensus on certain basics. In bilaterals and multilaterals of this sort, official "texts and traditions" are the criteria, and these are indeed in place in both cases. The Lutheran-Reformed Coordinating Committee for the current proposal clarified further the consensus in its Formula of Agreement just this year, using references to common Christian teaching cited in an earlier North American Lutheran-Reformed document, *Invitation to Action*, voted on in the 1980s by the national assemblies of all participating Reformed and most of the Lutheran antecedent bodies.

However, the critics are right to point to the disparity between what is declared officially and what is held functionally. But the charge must go much deeper than anecdotal reports that single out one denomination (reports that do not take account of the current vigorous movements of theological renewal in the UCC). The Search Institute's recent careful study of Christian teaching in six denominations does rate the United Church of Christ next to lowest in "Faith Maturity" and lowest in "Growth in Faith Maturity." At the same time, the ELCA is rated the very lowest in "Faith Maturity," and next to lowest in "Growth in Faith Maturity." We are all in the same boat, and there is no safe ecclesiastical harbor. As ELCA theologian George Lindbeck observes, his own church is "swayed by the same current fashions and is not better rooted in the historic faith" (*Lutheran Forum* 28, no. 1, p. 12).

What this dissonance between proclamation and practice means in full communion negotiations is the need to attend carefully to the second stage of bilateral agreements, variously called "actualization," "reception" or "realization." Often an acknowledgment of the complexity of procedures entailed or a recognition of institutional lethargy, it is also a discretionary act that recognizes today's theological diversity and new localisms. Actualization of this bilateral, or any others current, is appropriate only when and where congregations and judicatories do, in fact, affirm what is professed to be the case in the official agreement. To ascertain such, or grow toward such, can be a sobering recognition of reality, and more important, a teaching moment in Christian basics for the congregations and clergy of all the partner churches.

2. Are the participating churches really open to admonition about the limitations of their own tradition? Disagreement on the Eucharist is a case in point, and along with it the related diversity in patterns of worship and piety.

Commitment to mutual learning means that the Reformed must understand that another member of the Reformation family has had to remind it of the inseparability of Christ and his body, a Presence pervading its life, focal in the visibilities of a symbol-laden worship and definitive in the tangibilities of bread and wine. And that witness to the "haveable" entails legitimate Lutheran concerns about dissolution of the promise of Christ to be among us, as in Reformed flirtation with a "memorialism" that reduces the Eucharist to the recollection of a past event, or patterns of worship awash in religious subjectivities.

In turn, Lutherans must understand that mature Reformed teaching on the Lord's Supper (in its confessions, catechisms, statements of faith and sacramental liturgies) affirms unambiguously the real Presence but does so in its characteristic idiom of sovereignty, its language of "spiritual Presence" referring to the work of the Spirit in bringing the believer, in eating and drinking, into communion with the glorified humanity of Christ. In view of this, Lutherans may see how the Reformed witness to sovereignty (and worry about its dissolution) is expressed not only in eucharistic teaching and practice (the humanity of the elements, which can be grape juice as well as wine) but in comparable restraint in the use of symbols of the "haveable." Lutherans may also note the historic prominence of the pulpit and the sermon through which we are reminded of the divine freedom *over* us.

3. How can there be "interchange of clergy" given our different standards for the ordination and calling of clergy? Often the neuralgic point is the issue of openly gay and lesbian pastors. The ELCA faces this question with both its proposed full communion partners, Episcopal and Reformed. After the recent decision in the Righter case that judgment on such is not prescribed by the "common core" of Episcopal doctrine, ECUSA circumstances are not unlike those in the United Church of Christ, where regional or local option and sharp division of opinion play out in diversity of practice. In each church, whatever national resolutions are passed—one way or the other—Episcopal and UCC congregations will have latitude in decision-making.

Two things are germane in responding to this question. One of them is the premise written into the Formula of Agreement that whatever clergy interchange might take place (there is little evidence in any church of a move toward such) must be done "in orderly exchange," according to the norms of ordained ministry observed in the participating churches, standards that will not be set aside. The agreement does not require a congregation or judicatory in one church to accept a pastor if that pastor does not meet the first church's standards for doctrine and behavior.

A second has to do with the gift and admonition brought by the respective Lutheran and Reformed traditions. In three of the bodies with which the ELCA has been in quest for full communion (all shaped by the Reformed tradition)—the Episcopal Church, U.S.A., the United Church of Christ and the Presbyterian Church, U.S.A.—the issue of ordaining practicing gays and lesbians is a newly "disputed question." While the Presbyterian Church, U.S.A. has just passed a measure whose import is the exclusion of openly gay and lesbians persons from leadership positions, the closeness of the presbytery vote, the complexity of enforcement procedures, and the announcement of planned noncompliance by a significant number of congregations and clergy assure its being a continuing controverted issue in that church as well. The status of this newly disputed question as one in which devout Christians disagree can be understood as an expression of the *semper reformanda* of Reformed churches that requires the scrutiny, ever and again, of tradition—accountable as it is to the sovereign Word, Jesus Christ.

What would "mutual admonition" mean here? Would it entail a Lutheran acknowledgment that somewhere in the church catholic a critic-in-residence is needed, one that presses us to reexamine inherited positions, albeit always under the Word? Would it also require a Reformed acknowledgment that this matter is still a disputed question for which there is yet no "mind of the church," one needing continuing conversation within the whole body, *including* the stewards of a long moral tradition (i.e., the Lutheran *capax* making it the custodian of that tradition on just this subject)? Mutual admonition is risky business for all concerned. Particularly so for those on either side of the question who would make opinion on this matter the litmus test of faithfulness, ironically allowing a culture-war issue rather than a doctrinal basic to define the church's identity.

Conclusion
Some say the traditional ecumenical moves of mainline churches, such as the Lutheran-Reformed agreement, are obsolete and even boring, the frontier moving instead toward new unities with Christians outside the present ecumenical movement. But is this an either/or? The intense cyberspace debates and lively journalistic attention to the bilaterals, and the volatility of the issue in most of the participating churches, tells another story. Further, in Europe and beyond significant advances continue in a comparable 1973 Leuenberg Concord that brought into full communion eighty Lutheran and Reformed national churches, the counterpart to date in the United States being the UCC's 1981 full communion with the European Evangelical Church of the Union. Related to the apparent durability of such bilaterals is the fact that all serious ecumenism

will have someday to venture structural and governance decisions of the kind being risked in the Formula of Agreement and the Concordat and in multilaterals like COCU.

Beyond these facts and forecasts, an important opportunity in pedagogy is at stake in these kinds of ecumenical negotiations. In-depth study of basic issues like those demanded by this bilateral could press laity and clergy to levels of theological struggle about Christian basics desperately needed in these pluralist days. Such mind-stretching and soul-searching done in an admonitory framework would surely make for a catholicity of faith commensurate with the fullness of the body of Christ, and with it a thirst for a wider ecumenism with its own waiting charisms.

Part IV
The Search for
the Center in
Ethics & Institutions

In this section, learnings from church involvement in twentieth-century struggles are sought and simplistic culture-war options are rejected. A neglected intrainstitutional Christian witness is laid alongside the standard counterinstitutional and parainstitutional approaches in the first essay. How preaching can deal with the inflamed issue of abortion is then taken up. The twentieth-century wisdom of Reinhold Niebuhr is drawn upon for facing twenty-first-century issues in another chapter. The final piece examines the study of an evangelical seminary and a mainline seminary with a view to "restoring the center."

11

IBM & the
Incognito Christ[†]

"IBM" EQUALS *INSTITUTIONS,* MOLDERS OF THE NEXT MILLENNIUM. THEIR people are in our pews—the computer specialist third row center aisle, the second vice president two seats to the right, the assembly line worker over on the left. It might be Digital, Magee Hospital, First National, State University, even the Teamsters. And, of course, in the graying mainline, countless retirees, and in our downsizing economy, the unemployed worker, all of whom can tell you more than you want to know about the molding and the molded.

As we live through an era whose conventional wisdom measures all things by the bottom line, church activists fear the worst from institutions—economic, political and social. Aren't they the architects of the new lean and mean times? When they are winning, the poor, the unemployed, the overworked, the hungry, the homeless, the marginalized are the losers. Where are the comrades who will take on these "principalities and powers" as we did in the civil rights

[†]This essay was commissioned by the Greenleaf Center as research on the theology of institutions, 1995.

and peace movements of another day?

As echoed in the above, two assumptions have marked many of the movements for social change in which mainline churches have participated in this century: (1) The "establishment," a.k.a. the major economic, political and social institutions of American society, is the problem. (2) "Humanization," "liberation," "justice" will come about when it is called to account by organized efforts—political, economic and social. One result has been the regnant literature of social justice and the standard social action programs of the denominations.

The mainline churches *have* made a difference in the social history of North America, based on these *counterinstitutional* premises and strategies. Demonstrations, voter registration drives, letter-writing campaigns, boycotts, lobbying, civil disobedience . . . have been effective instruments of social change, as Martin Luther King Jr. taught a generation. May this continue to be so. Political fundamentalism, with quite another agenda, has learned these lessons well, underscoring the importance of an alternative witness of this kind.

We make a mistake, however, in thinking that this is the only avenue of institutional encounter. Historically, two others have played their part in social change. (1) A *parainstitutional* witness—the church itself as a parallel institution: here Christians decline the attempt directly to change the institutional givens, creating instead an alternative community of how the world should work, one *outside* and on the margins of society. The left-wing Reformation churches are known for this option, and today's "resident alien" proposals are kindred in spirit. (2) An *intrainstitutional* encounter in which change is sought from *within* the economic, political and social structures.

Is there reason to exclude any of these? Is there a ripe time—a *kairos*—for one or the other? Is there a way to incorporate learnings from the others while focusing on one approach?

Intrainstitutional Witness

To ignore the presence of IBM in our churches, or dismiss it ideologically, is to miss an opportunity for *intrainstitutional* social witness in a time so decisively shaped by these powers and principalities. The woman in the third row and the man two seats over might well prove to be among the most important agents of change in this kind of culture.

Over half a century ago H. Richard Niebuhr devised his durable typology of church/world encounter in *Christ and Culture*. He sought to ferret out both the strengths and weaknesses of each of the five types: "Christ against culture," "Christ of culture," "Christ above culture," "Christ and culture in paradox," "Christ transforming culture," suggesting the need for a pluriform approach, albeit the timeliness of one or another, and his own preference for the fifth type. The three institutional strategies noted here, with their obvious affinities to one or another of Niebuhr's types, invite the same kind of critical collegiality and question of *kairos*. Here we make an argument for that companionship, but for the special timeliness of *intrainstitutional* encounter.

What would that witness look like—in practice? And in theory? Two examples, and then their theological rationale.

In 1982, Eliot Church, UCC of Newton, Massachusetts, took a leaf from the post-World War II European "evangelical academies" and the mandate of the Andover Newton Laity Project of which it was a part. It challenged, vocationally, one fairly numerous segment of its congregation, its scientists: examine your workplace ministry, and do it together. In the ensuing years, down to the present day, from ten to fifteen men and women who work in companies on Route 128, in Boston universities and hospitals (among them a recent Nobel prize recipient) gathered each month with their pastor, the Rev. Herbert Davis, and a teacher, myself, to explore the meaning of secular ministry. Testing christological images and concepts emerging from the Center's studies (to be discussed below), they asked: What does the "prophetic office" require in the commercialization of gene research? In the making of "smart bombs"? What "priestly work" is entailed in corn research that can feed populations in underdeveloped countries? In the development of a code of ethics for cancer research personnel? What "royal ministry" goes on in the cost-benefits of cleaning up Boston Harbor? Each person, taking a turn on the "hot seat," brings a vocational issue to the group, with all the moral ambiguities attendant to ministry in today's institutions, and thus with a form of Luther's "third sacrament" of "mutual conversation and consolation" of the whole people of God. Eliot Church has found a small and still stumbling way "to equip the saints for the work of ministry" (Eph 4:12) amidst the powers, and thus to work intrainstitutionally for change.

Can institutions themselves have a ministry—not only individuals, but institutions *as such?* Tom Henry of Landry Cycle thinks so. Here a whole new landscape of intrainstitutional engagement opens up. We have few clues as to what this new frontier means.

More than a small-scale variation on "Ben and Jerry" do-gooding, this new fast-expanding company (now thirty-eight workers in two stores and a warehouse facility) frames its purpose and work in theological categories. If all ministry is Christ's ministry, then it must have something to do with an *institutional* prophetic, priestly and royal office. CEO Henry and his coworkers have sought to reflect this threefoldness in the lingo of the workplace: "quality and service," "teamwork," "productivity." Thus the exhausting and often chaotic labor of bicycle maintenance and repair—involving more than 1,000 parts—is carried out with a common institutional goal: Because what we do humanizes our world, quality and customer are foremost; Landry thus defines itself as a "house of hospitality." This, in a sense, is Landry's prophetic vision. But the focus on visionary goals has to be balanced by the welfare of unstinting employees who are drawn to the company by its vision. Thus a second institutional mandate and ministry: to honor the personhood and needs of the workers, to give them a share in company decision-making—the priestly office. And these two concerns cannot be dissociated from the financial facts of life: institutional viability, decisions by a "servant leadership" that must also take into account bottom-line realities—the royal office.

When an institution undertakes to execute all three ministries, it soon enough discovers their shadow side in a fallen world. Landry is a showcase for the ambiguities of institutional ministry. The vision of quality and customer service, of dedicated employees working long hours and attending intimately to each browsing cyclist, collides with employee needs for family life and leisure and income commensurate with those needs. The result is the running conversation among Landry managers and workers on how to keep the balance, not letting any one institutional ministry overwhelm the others. Hence the corporate grieving process over the loss of a valued colleague who had caught the vision but also required a better wage. Hence also the Landry "renewal day" for its workforce, taken off in midseason to honor the gift of ministry in all workers and their families as *persons* (in contrast to their utility as workers).

Theological Foundations

Enlisting the laity in our congregations in the struggle to recover and discover the ministry in and of institutions requires clear foundational principles. Marx spent years in the bowels of the British Museum working out his economic theories, and the theoreticians of capitalism based their work on Adam Smith's *Wealth of Nations.* Christians need their own foundational doctrine, a "theology of institutions." Some elements of such a theology are suggested by research done over fifteen years at Andover Newton on theological aspects of the ministry of the laity, and carried forward in new forms by the founder of its Center for the Ministry of the Laity, Richard Broholm.

Whatever else is meant by "powers and principalities," "authorities," "angels" and "demons," a strong case can be made for Scripture's acknowledgment of their social, political and economic underside. A vast literature that began in this century in the struggle against Nazism and "German Christianity" (Karl Barth, Hendrikus Berkhof et al.) continues to this day, most fruitfully in Walter Wink's trilogy on "the powers" *(Naming the Powers, Unmasking the Powers, Engaging the Powers).* Wink contends that what we experience as institutions— enduring social cohesions of structure, rules and practices with a life of their own—has something to do with the powers brought to be by God through the Word and the Spirit in the purposes of creation. But there is a mysterious More to "powers and principalities" not dealt with sufficiently in Wink's psychosocial analysis.[1] Wink has helped us understand the biblical world as the habitat of *powers* as well as *persons.* They too are part of the divine plan, brought to be by the Word of God, Jesus Christ, and indeed intimately related to the purposes of Christ, as in Colossians 1:16.

We must dig a little deeper to discern the "purposes of Christ." A long tradition in Christian teaching speaks of the continuation of Jesus Christ's ministry in the earthly body of Christ, the church. As Christ's original ministry (*diakonia*—service) among us was three-fold—described as "prophetic, priestly and royal" in Reformation, Roman Catholic and Eastern Orthodox theology and catechesis, and highlighted in Calvin's *Institutes*—so his present ministry takes this triple form. The prophetic ministry has been seen to continue in the church's preaching and teaching, the priestly in worship, prayer and sacrament, and the royal in its leadership roles and responsibilities. While too often confined to the pastoral office, ecumenical Christianity—from the Reformation catechisms to the Decree on the Apostolate of the Laity of the Second Vatican Council—holds that all three ministries belong to the *whole people of God*. And for almost fifty years now, in these same circles, "the ministry of the laity" has become a refrain in ecumenical documents (BEM and COCU), affecting even the translation of Scripture (for example, in the RSV and subsequent versions dropping "the fatal comma" in Ephesians 4:12, which alters "some pastors and teachers, to equip the saints, for the work of ministry" to "some pastors and teachers, to equip the saints for the work of ministry").

In the threefold office of Christ and our raised awareness about its manifestation in the ministries of the whole people of God are the beginnings of a "theology of institutions." But we are not there yet. Much of the inherited understanding of the ministry of the laity has been in a churchly and personal framework. Where are your gifts and ministries needed? How about the choir, or the diaconate, or even the social action committee? Maybe even serving on a denominational board? These are certainly valid questions and good directions. We need laity for these ministries. And more. As our church bulletins put it: "Ministers: all the congregation." And that means a ministry out there in *daily life*, not just in the church. All this is to the good.

The missing piece in our present understanding of the ministry of the laity is *institutional*. We have yet to incorporate the reality of the "powers"—created, fallen and redeemed—in which the 99 percent of the church called "the laity" live and work and are called to ministry. And *even further:* if the powers and principalities are created under and for Christ, then do not these very powers and principalities themselves also have a ministry? Indeed a prophetic, priestly and royal work? Powers, as well as persons, have been created, have fallen, have been preserved, then redeemed, and finally will be restored in the kingdom to come! Powers as well as persons are therefore *called,* called to a threefold ministry account-able to the sovereignty of God and the rule of Jesus Christ.

In the story of the Emmaus road, Christ keeps company with the disciples, but they do not recognize him (Lk 24:13-35). Only later, "in the breaking of bread," does he make himself known. So too in Matthew 25:31-46, Christ is present, but unknown, in circumstances of hunger, pain, estrangement, imprisonment. In both cases we hear a clear Word about *Christ incognito:* a hidden and unbidden Christ who comes among us. Indeed, the Matthew account suggests an unannounced presence in circumstances we would now call "insti-tutional"—in prisons, places of care (or the absence of care) for the sick and lonely; in economies of hunger, thirst and nakedness. And why not? If the institutional powers belong to Christ, why would their Creator, Preserver, Judge and Redeemer not be there among them? Commissioning us for ministries to, in and through them? Calling these very powers to their own proper ministry? As Christ's ministry continues in this new age of his rising and rule, so he is present incognito among the "thrones and authorities" as their Lord. And he claims the "church scattered" within their spheres to be stewards of that accountability.

Discerning the Signs of Christ's Presence

How would Christ amidst the powers be discerned? He comes not known and self-identified as in the church's Word and worship, but as hidden in secular terrain and under secular terms. The answer must be: wherever the threefold office of Christ continues. Histori-cally, the focus has been on these ministries *within* the body of Christ—the church *gathered* for proclamation (prophetic), worship and sacrament (priestly), and leadership (royal) ministries, all car-ried out in "servant style." But also, from latter-day Reformation to present-day Roman Catholic documents and commitments, the same Christ is acknowledged to be present in the body of Christ *scattered*—sent *outside* to their vocations in this world, the ministry of the whole people of God in work and play, home and school, life and death—persons in ministry in secular institutions. And now we are beginning to see that these institutions in which Christ is *also* present—incognito—are powers in their own right themselves also called to ministry.

What of the latter ministry *of* the powers? Eighteen years ago, Jitsuo Morikawa, a leader in "Word and deed" evangelism, and Robert Greenleaf, an AT&T executive and organizational theorist, pressed this question. It was taken up by Richard Broholm, who along with David Specht and a team of organizational leaders associated with the Robert Greenleaf Center continues the research and experimentation on the ministry of and in institutions.

Broholm and Specht have sought to interpret the threefold office of Christ in workplace categories that seek to honor its biblical intentions. They hold that faithful institutions will have comparable secular "offices," as is fitting for the incognito Christ: an "office of purpose" that embodies the prophetic role of conceiving of futures for the institution alternative to present realities, with "truth telling" and justice as normative; an "office of identity" that embodies the priestly role, sensitizing the institution to the needs of all the "stakeholders" and the common good; an "office of stewardship" embodying the royal role of servant leadership, assuring the viability of the institution. The assumption throughout is that institutions as powers in the plan of God have a ministry coherent with the threefold work of the hidden Christ.

Aware that all institutions share in the universal Fall of creation, Broholm and Specht also speak of the "shadow side" of each office. A gift-ministry can be corrupted: the prophetic by utopianism, the priestly by sentimentality, the royal by the hegemony of the almighty dollar. Distortion comes about most often when an institution falls prey to reductionism, eliminating one or more of the offices.

The attempt to connect Christology to institutional realities in this fashion is a leap of theological imagination. A dangerous one, some will say. Finding Christ at work in, with and over IBM? You've secularized the sacred! Translating the prophetic office into the secular terms of "an office of purpose" and Landry's humanizing vision? A pretty tame version of Christ's radical claims. The care of "stakeholders" with a "renewal day"? What about a union to guarantee worker rights—the "prophetic" where you've settled only for the "priestly"? Letting the "bottom line" into the picture means letting Jesus bless Mammon!

Both the practitioners and theorists of workplace ministry struggle with all these questions, and many more like them. As soon as one ventures the *intrainstitutional* move in ministry, H. Richard Niebuhr's compromising "Christ *of* culture" type looms into view. Once you opt for being *in* the world, you run the risk of being *of* the world. That is why Dietrich Bonhoeffer has meant so much to those committed to the ministry of the laity in the workplace. Not only his call to "participate in the sufferings of God in the world," and hence secular ministry, but also his sober recognition that we can live there only by the grace of God, the mercy that evokes our penitence for compromise, and the power that both sustains us in and makes us restive with our ambiguities. And more, a full-orbed commitment to institutional ministry means colleagueship with *parainstitutional* mission and *counterinstitutional* mission, with their sharpened sensitivity to the call of "Christ *against* culture" and "Christ *transforming* culture," even as they need the alliance of an *intrainstitutional* ministry that runs the risks of life with Christ inside IBM.

Is a third frontier of social mission possible in our time and place? Could the countless laity commissioned in baptism for ministry be equipped by their congregations for *intrainstitutional* mission? What would that mean for them as individual ministries, and for their institutions *as* ministries? The jury is out. We are only at the beginning of testing both the theology and practice here suggested. Yet its day has come.

12

Preaching
on Abortion[†]

ABORTION, SPONTANEOUS OR INDUCED, IS ENDING FETAL LIFE BEFORE IT reaches full term.

Key questions in the debate on abortion are *When* is a fetus a human being? *What* are the circumstances, if any, under which abortion is a legitimate moral choice?

Preaching on this controversial issue requires familiarity with the range of opinion in the church and wider society on the two disputed questions.

Human beginnings. In past and present debate, human origins are placed at

1. fertilization—sperm and ovum join to create a zygote with its own genetic code

2. implantation—the embryo is implanted in the uterine wall, five to eight days after fertilization

3. segmentation and recombination—"twinning" (one egg that

[†]This essay is based on the entry "Abortion" (Dorothy Fackre, coauthor), in *Handbook for Preaching*, ed. James Cox (Louisville, Ky.: Westminster John Knox, 1992).

becomes two) and "mosaic" (two eggs that become one) are definitive, at fourteen days (fertilization, implantation and segmentation
have been variously identified as the point of "conception")

4. detectable heartbeat, at three to four weeks

5. discernible cerebral cortex, at approximately five weeks

6. formation—the fetus "looks human" and ultrasound technology shows movement, at six to seven weeks

7. readable brain waves, at eight weeks

8. quickening—the mother feels movement, at fourteen to twenty
weeks

9. viability—survivability outside the womb, at twenty to twenty-
eight weeks

10. birth—natural life begins outside the womb

Christian opinion on human beginnings has taken significant
shifts, as in the change in the traditional Roman Catholic view from
"quickening" to "conception," beginning in the eighteenth century.

A subquestion of political import is: Do human beginnings entail
"equal rights"? Some believe fetal personhood proceeds developmen-
tally, rights being determined by the stage of growth, with parity at
viability or birth. Others declare for equal rights at conception. Still
others defend fetal rights but give priority to maternal rights under
circumscribed conditions.

On reasons for abortion, perspectives within and beyond the
Christian community vary widely.

Roman Catholic moral teaching forbids "direct abortion." However, its "principle of double effect" holds that a pathological organ
that threatens the life of the mother can be removed, even though
the surgery results in "indirect abortion." Others allow for abortion
only when the mother's life is in peril, but do so without the limited
rationale of double effect.

An additional reason for abortion offered by another constituency
is peril to the health of the mother. Opinion is divided as to whether
this includes mental as well as physical health. In close proximity
are those who hold that other violations of the mother or breaches
of moral law, such as rape and incest, justify abortion.

Still other points of view focus on the perceived consequences to
the fetus, mother, family and wider society. Some believe birth into

a dehumanizing socioeconomic setting or a dysfunctional condition warrants termination of fetal life. Others contend that overpopulation justifies selective abortion. Still others hold that the fulfillment of a woman's personal goals takes precedence as a value and legitimates the removal of any reproductive barrier to that fulfillment.

Biblical Instances

Only two verses in Scripture refer directly to abortion. Exodus 21:22 (NRSV) requires a fine for persons who, while fighting, "injure a pregnant woman so that there is a miscarriage." (The following verse, Exodus 21:23, exacts heavier punishment for additional hurt: "If any harm follows, then you shall give life for life," implying a distinction between abortion and murder.) In Hosea 9:14 the author berates the people ("Ephraim") for their sins and entreats God to "give them a miscarrying womb and dry breasts."

As with some other doctrinal and ethical themes, theological reflection on abortion develops by inference from Scripture rather than by direct citation. Such texts can include the following.

Genesis 1:26-27 establishes the sanctity of human life made in the image of God. Matthew 1:18-23, Luke 1:31, John 1:14 and other passages on the Word made flesh suggest (as in the Orthodox tradition) that human life from conception forward is hallowed by the Incarnation. Jeremiah 1:4-5 and Luke 1:15 comment on the consecration of life before birth. Psalm 90:10, 1 Corinthians 13:12 and other passages on human finitude, and Romans 3:9-18 and other passages on human sin, imply that judgments on moral issues with no explicit directives in revelation should be made with a modesty appropriate to that ambiguity. Romans 3:21-29 and other passages on justification affirm that Christians live by grace and forgiveness in the midst of the shortfalls and unclarities of human decision-making. Psalm 82:3-4, Amos 4:1 and other passages on the "weak and needy" or those who "oppress the poor, who crush the needy," call for defense of the helpless. These suggest a concern for *both* the vulnerable fetus and women whose pregnancies are related to oppressive social circumstances.

Options for Preaching

Commentary should take its orientation from biblical indicators, recognize the variety of perspectives within the Christian community, and have due regard for the insights of human experience—from those most directly affected, from the conscience of the community, and from the status of scientific knowledge. With these reference points in mind a preacher can work with the following strategy when preaching about abortion.

Ground assertions in the biblical warrants for human dignity. Important here is the classical teaching that humans are made in the image of God (Gen 1:26-27). Sanctity is conferred on each by virtue of this special relation of God to the human order, climaxing in the Word made flesh (Jn 1:14).

Explore the affirmation of human sanctity in the light of the New Testament's description of the Incarnation. As the Holy Spirit brings Christ into solidarity with the human race at conception (Mt 1:18-23), fetal life is dignified from its beginnings. Yet the angels sing, the shepherds kneel, and the star shines at Jesus' birth (Mt 2:1-2; Lk 2:6-10). Accordingly, Christmas is the high festival of Christ's coming. This distinction between the days of conception and nativity points to a difference between a human being as a fetus and a human being at birth. So too, Exodus 21:22-23 makes a distinction between human beingness as a fetus and human beingness as an adult.

Show the relation of decision-making on abortion to choices made on other moral questions in which reality factors (finitude and sin) regularly qualify the perfect or literal execution of absolutes.

When the life of the fetus is pitted against the life of the mother, abortion is recognized, even by most "prolife" advocates, as a legitimate choice and the lesser of two evils. Implicit in this judgment is the distinction between human beingness and full human beingness.

The church is currently struggling to clarify the conditions under which the sanctity of the bearer might take precedence over the sanctity of the fetus. In addition to peril to the life and health of the mother, rape and incest are increasingly cited as evils of sufficient warrant for a "just abortion." Beyond that there is no developing "mind of the church." Defense of the weak is adduced by both prolife and prochoice positions. Partisans also warn about the corruptibility of power by those who wield it over the fetus or over the woman who bears it.

The conscience burdened with a painful abortion choice must hear from the church the word of forgiveness and justifying grace (Rom 3:21-29) and experience the support of the community of forgiven sinners (Acts 2:42-47).

Make clear the varied opinions in church and culture on the point of human beginnings and the influence of the state of science on the same. (Current data on segmentation and recombination indicate that individual humanness cannot be settled until the fourteenth day after fertilization, which suggests this as the point of conception.) A preacher can also call for modesty in Christian assertions about origins, given their dependence on shifting scientific data.

Show how abortion decisions are inextricable from institutional patterns. As such, Christians have a right and duty to implement their convictions in political action and legislation. (Ex 21:22-23 is an ancient civil code.) However, in a pluralistic society, they must not force their biblically grounded views on the public but press instead the points of convergence with the community's conscience (as in the civil rights struggle in the 1960s).

Where abortion is widespread its relation to social, economic and educational deprivation is unmistakable. The church has a responsibility to address these contextual factors ("creatureliness") and also avoid a moralism insensitive to predisposing circumstances.

Comprehensive church education in sexuality is a necessary complement to institutional witness.

13

The Continuing Relevance of Reinhold Niebuhr[†]

THEOLOGIANS COME AND GO. A TRIP THROUGH THE SECOND-HAND SECTION of a theological bookstore is evidence enough of the transiency of most, even the once-heralded bestseller. Theologians come and go, but now and then one endures. In this concluding section, we speak of the "durable," a counterpoint to the opening chapter's "ephemeral."

Why has Reinhold Niebuhr proved *durable?* Alan Paton had this opinion: "I think him to be the wisest man I ever knew, with an understanding of human nature and human society that no one has equaled in our century."[1] Perhaps that is why an article in a recent Lutheran journal asks, "Niebuhr for the 90s?"[2] and a recent feature in the *Christian Century* reviews a new outpouring of books on Niebuhr.[3] And why yet another biography of Niebuhr, Richard Fox's, for all its errors and distortions, received such attention. (As important as any of these are Charles Brown's *Niebuhr and His Age* and his *Reinhold Niebuhr Reader,* among the best of the books on Niebuhr's

---

[†]This essay was given as one of the 1997 Niebuhr Lectures, Elmhurst College, Illinois.

life and thought.)[4] I want to make a case for "Niebuhr for the 90s" by following Paton's leads: showing how his astute social ethics and political analysis are grounded in his understanding of human nature and destiny—a matter, finally of his *theology*.

Often it is the novelist or historian that understands better the theological Niebuhr. Arthur Schlesinger Jr. echoes Paton in a recent *New York Times* op-ed tribute to Niebuhr:

> He persuaded me and many of my contemporaries that original sin provides a far stronger foundation for freedom and self-government than illusions about human perfectibility. . . . His warnings against utopianism, messianism and perfectionism strike a chord today. We are beginning to remember what we should never have forgotten: we cannot play the role of God to history, and we must strive as best we can to attain decency, clarity and proximate justice in an ambiguous world.[5]

Niebuhr as Christian teacher and preacher is the undergirding of Niebuhr the ethicist and political philosopher. We need his wisdom today as it provides critical perspective on current *theological* alternatives. Of course, Niebuhr has his shortcomings, but there are durable solidities among the ephemeralities.

The Biblical Drama

Niebuhr's continuing theological witness has to do with his grasp of "the big picture," his portrayal of the sweep of God's relations with the world—the "biblical drama," as he calls it, with some debt to the "biblical theology" movement of his day. He traces it out in conversation with, and critique of, other perspectives in his magnum opus, *The Nature and Destiny of Man*, the Gifford Lectures given in 1940 to the sound of falling bombs along the nearby Scottish seacoast. In the biblical drama, Niebuhr anticipates one kind of current "narrative theology," the one that speaks first and foremost not of our personal or social stories, nor even of biblical stories, but of Scripture's Grand Narrative that runs from creation to consummation, with its center point in Jesus Christ. Yes, the biblical epic, but also the church's tale, a community story set forth in its historic creeds and confessions and its most current corporate testimonies.

Creation

We begin with chapter 1, *creation*. Scripture's ancient accounts of the world's beginnings that Niebuhr believed spoke profundities about which alternative perspectives, secular and religious, were innocent. Not about the penultimate "when, where and how" questions that are the proper business of the sciences, but about the ultimate "why and what" issues. Such saga (Niebuhr, following the day's intellectual conventions, called it "myth"), about a garden with a talking snake and a walking God, are to be taken seriously but not literally.

Niebuhr's counsels are timely as ever with regard to both the form and the substance of his interpretation of chapter 1 of the biblical story. In the first case—the form—he has a word to speak to the loud partisans of biblical inerrancy so vocal in church disputes today, whose litmus test for faithfulness is the historical accuracy of the creation accounts, a paradoxically modernist historiography that fails to understand the poetic and theological genre and thus misses the deep message embedded in the text.

The second case—the substance, the message—has implications for a range of issues, ecological, political and philosophical. The Christian *doctrine* of creation inherent in and developed out of this chapter in the story holds (1) that the world, created by God, is thereby good, but not God, and (2) that the self-transcending and self-directing part of a good nature, *human* nature, is, as such, the very "image of God" albeit immersed in nature's "contingencies and necessities." Thus, ecologically, because of the goodness but not Godness of creation, nature while not worshiped must be honored and stewarded for the purposes of God, not ravaged in self-serving human agendas—capitalist, Marxist or otherwise. Thus, politically, because human nature is inextricable from nature in bodiliness and socioeconomic nexus, we must struggle to make just the social and economic arrangements that impact the enfleshed and socially shaped souls of human beings.

All of this is a sharp challenge to dualistic religions and theologies that denigrate the natural world and/or angelistic anthropologies that ignore the human body and its entanglements. On the other hand, it challenges today's determinisms and naturalisms that fail to acknowledge the freedom of the human spirit and the unique dignity of human beings made in the divine image. It is worlds away, also, from the kind of "New Age" notions on the fusion of deity and humanity which lead one New Age guru to conclude, more or less logically, that "we are gods and might as well get good at it." This latter judgment takes us quite naturally to Reinhold Niebuhr on the second chapter of the biblical story: "the Fall."

The Fall

For many commentators, this chapter is the heart of the theological Niebuhr, accounting for the description of his view as "Christian realism." Is he not the chief twentieth-century poser of Karl Menninger's question, *Whatever Became of Sin?* Certainly a sober, indeed somber anthropology is one of Niebuhr's greatest contributions. But he was able to look into the abyss only because he had lifted his eyes over its rim to see a horizon beyond it. Or to put it narratively, it was the radical resources from subsequent chapters of the Story—its christological center and eschatological closure—that enabled him both to discern and to deal with the seriousness of human sin.

On the Fall: again, Niebuhr wants to retrieve the theological riches from a Genesis tale either dismissed as superstitious fable or wrongly defended as literal history. Through Augustinian-Reformation lenses, he saw there the universal human *No!* to the divine invitation, the Adamic will to play God. The centering of the self in itself is the primal sin of pride, *hubris,* Luther's incurvedness of the self into itself, Kierkegaard's shut-upness.

This self-idolatry, "vertically" before God, plays out "horizontally" in human relationships, according to Niebuhr, in the arrogance of the powerful—powerful in every sense of the word—including the wise, the righteous and the holy, as well as those with political, economic and social power—the "lording it over" the weak and vulnerable. But given the duality of human nature—the limitations of our creatureliness as well as the self-transcendence of the *imago,* our finitude as well as our freedom—the primal sin of pride *coram Deo* expresses itself not only in the abuse of our freedom but also in the apathy of an irresolute will, an "escape" from freedom into sensuality and what the monks called acedia—lassitude, torpor.

(Here Niebuhr's feminist critics are both right and wrong—right that he reads the Fall from a masculine perspective, seeing it essentially as the pride of the powerful, not giving adequate attention to the comparable risk of flight from power; but wrong in [a] failing to see that for Niebuhr there are *two* meanings of "pride"—the second being the root sin of self-glorification that lies underneath both arrogance and apathy, which cannot be ignored by any who take the persistence of sin seriously; [b] missing the place he does give to the twin sin of apathy, the "escape from freedom" and sense of self; and [c] elevating the importance of self-assertion for the powerless to the point of obscuring their corruptibility and equating victimhood with virtue.)

Into this interpretation of the story of the Fall, Niebuhr imported a Kierkegaardian-derived existentialist analysis that saw a universal anxiety attendant to human life "at the juncture of nature and spirit," our ambiguous locus sharing finitude with the animals and freedom with the angels. In such an analysis, we resolve the tension by the will to self-security and self-idolatry that in turn manifests itself in either the arrogance of power or the flight into powerlessness.

While the existentialist account may be a creature of a post-World War II problematic ruminated upon variously by Heidegger, Sartre, Camus, Marcel and Tillich, and superseded by the quandaries of other times and places, the biblical insights about the mystery of iniquity anterior to the existentialist analysis are perduring.

At end-of-century we are faced with the same kind of illusions about human nature that Niebuhr targeted in his own time:

For one, Niebuhr would have sharp words for today's "Christian Right." While he would respect it for seeking to relate the gospel to the political arena, in contrast to the apolitical fundamentalisms of his own day, he would judge it innocent of the radical biblical teaching that understands the persistence of sin in the life of the redeemed. The transport of the sharp before-and-after evangelical experience of new birth into the world of politics—saints here and sinners over there—creates a Manichaean "us-and-them" mentality and strategy that (a) leaves no place for self-criticism within its own ranks, (b) fails to see the ambiguities in every political judgment and (c) obscures the merits in whatever "evil empire" it battles. Such sharp juxtapositions do produce the political energy for which the

Christian Right is known (comparable to the evangelistic zeal of conservative evangelicals). However, the absence of self-critical principle or piety leads rather predictably to the seductions of "money, sex and power," of the kind that felled the political-fundamentalist "televangelists" in the 1980s. Where the evil is seen to be in "them" and sanctity in "us," and where this is raised to apocalyptic levels and given access to levers of political power, the temptation and fall of the powerful should not be surprising. Where no lessons are learned from these waves of uncritical piety, more of the same can be expected.[6] When such a fall comes, and unrealistic self-definitions and expectations are shattered, the danger of despair and retreat is also predictable—the demise of arrogance giving rise to its twin, apathy.

Niebuhr would find himself uneasy about another point of view at the other end of the theological and political spectrum, the neopacifisms so ardently argued by a Stanley Hauerwas or a John Yoder. Niebuhr would respect their commitment to the absolutes of New Testament love, a stewardship of the eschatological vision always needed in the church—as in the role of the pacifist churches as critics-in-residence of both church and society—because love *is* the final law of life holding the world accountable to who God is, what Christ was and what the redeemed world will someday be, exposing its shortfall and pressing it to closer approximations. At the same time, neopacifism's perfectionist ethic assumes far too much about the possibilities of achieving its ends in the Christian life and community or in the wider society. As such, it produces a sectarian ecclesiology that (a) withdraws the church from the push and pull of the political struggle, with all the necessary compromises attendant thereto; (b) ignores the social role of latent violence in a fallen world (police, law and the courts) that sets civil bounds to human sin; and (c) flirts with the same naiveté and self-righteousness within its own ranks that attends the us-and-them militants of the Christian Right.

In the sharp lines drawn between the faithful remnant and the fallen world, neopacifism also discounts the applicability of worldly counsel in matters of what Niebuhr calls the "nicely calculated less and more" of political judgment. This leads to the third chapter of the biblical story.

Covenant—with Noah

Niebuhr strongly believed that even in a fallen world, God "has not left himself without a witness" (Acts 14:17), that alien forces are used by the divine hand—"Assyria as the rod of God's anger." This meant that while the final Word is spoken by God in Christ, the divine freedom can raise up from stones, "children of Abraham." Because this is so, we cannot disdain a wider worldly wisdom wherever the divine hand chooses to distribute it, in political strategies, economic counsels, historical analyses, philosophical ruminations or even universal human sensibilities of right and wrong. All these are always accountable, however, to the defining disclosure in Jesus Christ. This made for borrowings by Niebuhr from secular insight, and the defense of Christian faith based on its tangents with human experience and discernments (a modest apologetics), and also a recognition of truths in other religions beyond the special history of God with Israel and in Christ.

The warrants for all this Niebuhr sometimes traced to the view of the *imago* as damaged but not destroyed, and other times in a doctrine of general revelation, one not limited to the Creator God but to the presence of a "hidden Christ" in the secular world. In our narrative framework, it is better located after the Fall as a grace of preservation, the "common grace" of Niebuhr's Reformed tradition released through the "covenant with Noah." Here God sets a rainbow over the path to let the human journey—the Great Story—go forward, giving a dim awareness of its destination. If we borrow the language of the Jewish tradition with which Niebuhr had great affinities, those outside the special covenant are the "Noachides" of general covenant.

The relevance of this chapter enables Christians to honor the true, the good, the holy and the beautiful wherever they appear, and to give God the glory. It supports interreligious dialogue (but with succeeding chapters does not fall into relativism); it learns from the moral insight and passion for justice and peace in secular movements and persons, encourages appreciation for and conversation with the arts and sciences, and welcomes wisdom where found in philosophies past and present, all of which can serve as corrective to the errors and omissions of the church, and prompt a search into its own lore for things that it has obscured.

Niebuhr's relevance here is a needed counterpoint to other kinds of narrative theology that tend to reduce the biblical story to Jesus stories or to the holy history from exodus to Easter. Wary of the camel's nose in the tent—that any concession to a "point of contact" external to Christ leads to the captivity of the church and faith to cultural ideologies—today's Barth-shaped theologies rightly affirm a christocentric faith but wrongly deny the biblical testimony to this chapter in the story, one witnessed to by the virtually unanimous voice of the Christian tradition. At the same time, Niebuhr rejects the reduction of the biblical story to this one chapter, as in contemporary theologies that hold Christian faith hostage to philosophical systems, political and economic ideologies, psychological and social theories, scientific or mystical cosmologies, and inflations of truth fragments given to us by covenant with Noah. How to relate but not capitulate to the best the world has to offer . . . how to make eclectic, not totalistic use of these glimpses of truth . . . this is the continuing challenge. (Indeed, in spite of the sharp disagreement between Niebuhr and Barth on just this chapter of the Story, it is interesting that in his later years [IV/3/1] Barth gave more attention to the matter, attempting to honor the wisdom of the world as what he came to call "free communications" and "parables of the Kingdom," albeit within his well-known "actualist" framework.)[7]

Covenant—with Israel

In his later years, Niebuhr shocked many Niebuhrians when he declared that while he believed Christian faith to be the final truth, he opposed the conversion of Jews. In this respect Niebuhr anticipated some forms of what is today called "antisupersessionism," the belief that God's special covenant in Jesus Christ does not abrogate God's special covenant with the Jewish people.

There are a variety of forms of antisupersessionism, ones that run from a political dispensationalism that ardently supports the claims of the Jewish state on the grounds of a literalist eschatology, to highly relativist views of religion that hold Judaism is right for Jews, Christianity right for Christians, Islam right for Muslims, and so on. Niebuhr did not work out clearly his own view but did assert, in Romans 9—11 fashion, the special chapter of God's dealings with

Israel and its continuing legitimacy, especially so the witness of its prophetism and the rightful need after the Holocaust of a Jewish nation state.

Niebuhr's relevance here is his refusal to dissolve this covenant chapter of the story into either general revelation or special revelation in Christ, and his honoring of the prophetic tradition and its relevance to today's struggles. At the same time, he did not succumb to a relativism that would deny the particularity of truth in either Judaism or Christianity. I believe there are ways in Christian theology to maintain both the scandal of Christian particularity and the continuing covenant with Israel, but that is a large subject in its own right. For all that, here as elsewhere in his theology he managed to steer between the Scylla of imperialism and the Charybdis of relativism, again providing a wisdom that eludes the reductionists.

Jesus Christ
The Story goes on for Niebuhr past the previous chapter, for the Old Testament poses a problem it does not answer: the hope for the vindication of the righteous that yet must confront the prophetic discernment that even the righteous stand judged. The answer is given, for Niebuhr, on the cross—where the judgment that all deserve is received not by us but by God, in the passion and death of Jesus Christ. On Calvary God does not indulge sin but takes its consequences into the divine being and in suffering love bears the fallen world forward to its end in an undeserved mercy. Thus the same self-sacrificing *agapē* manifest in the life of Jesus acts on Golgotha to receive and display the costly divine forgiveness.

> The Christian doctrine of the Atonement, with its paradoxical conception of the relation of the divine mercy to the divine wrath, is the final key.[8]

Here is a messianism in which the Son of Man of the Jewish apocalyptic tradition and the suffering servant of Isaiah are brought together in Jesus' declaration that "the Son of Man must suffer." That the triumph of suffering love is real at the Story's center and will complete the incompletes of history at its closure is validated by the resurrection of Jesus Christ.

In traditional theological terms, Niebuhr here blends the doctrines of incarnation and atonement, for it is God as human who is the Person who does the at-one-ing Work of reconciliation. Niebuhr's "suffering God" theology is traceable to the influence of Donald Baillie, especially his work *God Was in Christ*.

Apart from the ethical import already glanced at here, the relevance of this Christology lies in Niebuhr's ability to resist the common reductionism in today's understandings of both the person and the work. Such tendencies reduce the person to either the human nature, as in a stream of liberal theologies, or the divine nature, as in a stream of conservative theologies, or in the reductionist atonement theologies that focus exclusively on one or another aspect of the multifaceted work of Christ—the Galilean example and teacher, the Calvary Savior, the Easter Lord or Bethlehem's incarnate one. The relevance lies, as well, in the more full-orbed piety associated with such a multifaceted Christology, one that finds a place for obedience to the Galilean Jesus and gratitude to the divine person and work for God's solidarity with us at Bethlehem, the mercy toward sinners granted on Calvary, and the victory over suffering and death on Easter morning. Further, while this special revelation in Christ cannot be derived from human experience and thus is "foolishness to the Greeks," it can illumine human experience, for it maintains the radical love of Christ as the norm necessary to drive us beyond our reliance on present achievements, exposing their ambiguity and posing the question to which the disclosure of the divine mercy in Christ speaks—enabling us to live with our shortfalls but at the same time to press beyond them.

Church

Niebuhr's understanding of the church was at best undeveloped and at worst deficient. One aspect of his understanding of the church does deserve mention, a clear carryover from his own Evangelical Synod and later his Evangelical and Reformed connections, in which no worship was complete without a corporate confession of sin and pastoral assurance of pardon. And this takes us to the next doctrine, soteriology—or more exactly, subjective soteriology, the chapter on personal salvation.

Salvation

As all Christian doctrine is interrelated, we have already touched on some of the features of this chapter, what Niebuhr called "the complexities in the spiritual life" of Christians, that is, the pilgrimage and paradox of grace, as traced by St. Paul and elaborated especially by Augustine, Luther and Calvin. The gospel is the good news of both "mercy toward" and "power in" those who believe. The sinner is exposed as sinner by the love of God in Christ and by the same love is declared accepted even though unacceptable, driven to repentance by the former and to faith by the latter. Yet true faith, in grateful obedience (Calvin), busy in love (Luther), is a power *in* us as well as a pardon *for* us, a grace imparted as well as imputed.

How relevant is all this? Its relevance *coram Deo* we will only learn someday as we stand before our Maker. But right now it can also give us a "serenity to accept" and a "courage to change," the pardon and power here discussed and now lived out in countless twelve-step programs that use Niebuhr's prayer and translate it into their own agendas. It meant for Niebuhr living by God's mercy rather than by the illusion of human righteousness, ours or others', a self-critical spirit in oneself, and a realism in human affairs. It also means, even with this sobriety, an impetus to strive for better things in oneself and in human affairs, and the power to do so—the "paradox of grace." Again, within the church and vis-à-vis other Christian alternatives, its relevance consists in walking the same tightrope without falling off into a quietism that makes no effort in self and society because all illusions have been lost, and an activism that still naively assumes an escalator of progress in both self and society.

Consummation

The last chapter of the Story is the consummation of all things. In contrast to theologies of history that look for a climax within history or above it, Niebuhr speaks of it as at "the end of history." Taking the biblical accounts of the world's endings, as he did its beginnings, "seriously, but not literally," he read them not as answers to the "when, where and how" questions but as testimony to the great what and why issues. So this declaration:

Some of us have been persuaded to take the stone that we then

rejected and make it the head of the corner. . . . There is no part
of the Apostles Creed which . . . expresses the whole genius of the
Christian faith more neatly than just the despised phrase, "I
believe in the resurrection of the body."[9]
As in the creed, Niebuhr clusters the great stained-glass windows that
portray the end, translucent but not transparent, letting in enough
light to make our own way but giving us no clear view of what is to
come: the return of Christ, final judgment, everlasting life.

The relevance of Niebuhr's interpretation of these themes continues to this day, providing us with a modest alternative to the lush
eschatological scenarios of apocalyptic fundamentalism, a hope that
assures us of the ultimate victory of the purposes of God that can
sustain us in the midst of historical defeats, and give us a vision of
the way the world should work that makes us restless with all the
givens—"your kingdom come on earth as it is in heaven"! Further,
the kind of this-worldly signs toward the coming reign of God are
suggested in the content of the End, an eschatology inseparable from
ethics: bodies are to be honored in accord with God's care for them
in the resurrection of the body; earth and its natural environment
are to be stewarded rightly given the "new heaven and new earth";
the structures of society are also here and now accountable to God,
for they will be a kingdom and a new Jerusalem; yet no achievement
in history can be equated with the new world to come, for Satan
appears even at the close of history.

The relevance of Reinhold Niebuhr's eschatology has to do not
only with the specifics of his interpretation of these great symbols
but also his counsel in veering us away from the twin eschatologies
that tempt us today: the trust that we can build the kingdom within
history and the resulting self-righteous fury and intolerance that
eventuate from those who must cling to this illusory hope, or the
eschatology that wants heaven now and cannot wait for God's good
time—whether it be the trendy neomysticisms that seduce people
away from historical responsibilities or the suicide cults that promise
immediate bliss by acts of self-violence.

Reinhold Niebuhr, where are you when we need you! Not only as
an astute observer of the political scene but as Christian theologian,
warts and all.

14

Seminary Cultures—
Evangelical & Mainline[†]

HANAUMA BAY IS A SNORKELER'S HEAVEN. HAWAII'S COLORFUL FISH SPECIES can only be discovered by "being there," by taking a plunge into the waters with mask and air tube. Similarly, the study *Being There* is a study in snorkeling, the results of a sustained swim in the underwater life of Protestant seminaries.

A team of church social scientists chose two species to track: "Evangelical" and "Mainline," understood to be in the "streams" of evangelicalism and mainline Protestantism. The identity of the schools, both described as large, secure and at the center not the extreme ends of their constituencies, is disguised. This work is a search for subsurface phenomena, "cultures" below the level of curriculum or conventional self-descriptions. Culture so understood is made up of "shared (publicly available) symbolic forms—world-views, beliefs, ritual practices, ceremonies, art and architecture, language and patterns of everyday interaction" (268), the "script" that guides the "actors" (5) in being there. The researchers immersed themselves for three seminary years (1989-1990 through 1991-1992) in the

[†]This review of *Being There: Culture and Formation in Two Theological Schools* by Jackson W. Carroll, Barbara G. Wheeler, Daniel O. Aleshire and Penny Long Marler (New York: Oxford University, Press, 1997) was written for the November-December 1998 issue of *Books & Culture*.

culture of each school, living for periods on campus; attending classes, chapels and trustee meetings; interviewing students, faculty, administration and staff; eating in the cafeterias, visiting related congregations, and listening in on campus conversations and controversies.

The research project was focused on how seminary culture shapes students, providing them with a "normative goal" and a "cultural tool kit." Learnings from the plunge are for seminary leadership but have implications also for other educational institutions and shed light on today's religious partisanships. Findings and judgments include the too-often unrecognized power of cultures in forming students both during and after their school years; the difficulty of institutional efforts to alter cultures; the importance of faculty in culture-formation; wariness about the proffered panaceas of new technology and marketing techniques; paideia as a worthy seminary goal. The influence of the ideas of Clifford Geertz, Ann Swidler, Peter Berger and Thomas Luckmann is acknowledged and evident throughout.

The report of this impressive research tells us not only about the institutions observed but also about the tacit culture the investigators bring to the inquiry. As Don Browning points out elsewhere, the "congregational studies" movement (which influenced this project) is "theory-laden" ("Congregational Studies as Practical Theology," in *American Congregations*, ed. James P. Wind and James W. Lewis [Chicago: University of Chicago Press, 1994], 2:192-221). Watching the watchers, therefore, is worth doing; in this case it includes a look at the snorkelers from the bluff over Hanauma Bay, a perch formed from my long-time acquaintance as a mainline outsider with the anonymous Evangelical Seminary (including a course taught there during the research period), some knowledge of Mainline and decades on the faculties of two comparable mainline seminaries. And yet, and yet . . . any confident talk of higher perspective—at sea level or above—must in turn be reminded that "he who sits in the heavens laughs" (Ps 2:4) at any claims to a God's-eye view.

What did researchers Jackson Carroll and Barbara Wheeler see in their swim through evangelical waters? Their report includes selected faculty profiles, descriptions of seminary "contests" (important ones during the research were "believer's baptism," seminary response to the appearance of well-known nonevangelical figures in a "modern theology" course, debates on the "Iron Sharpens Iron" student notice board, a running school controversy about the ordination of women), glimpses of representative students, and a study of the dynamics of the "inner circle" and "outer ring" of a women's dormitory. The backdrop to the stories is an institution that is nondenominational and heterogeneous in its degree programs; its study paths lead to both parochial and paraparochial ministries, and it attracts many students who arrive without denominational affiliation.

The "message" found to be central to Evangelical Seminary's culture is that

God's plan for the world and the redemption of human life is an orderly and responsible one that is inscribed in the Bible. The obligation of human beings, in return for the inestimable gift of salvation, is to learn that orderly plan and accept the grace that enables them to live by it. Secular society and liberal Christians who have ignored the biblical plan must be shown its superiority to the human-centered principles they have endorsed. Even more pressing, evangelical persons, agencies and churches most be recalled to observe God's covenantal plan; they have too often permitted the corrosion of modern technology and self-indulgent piety to undermine the necessary discipline and order of truly biblical faith. (204-5)

Evangelical, therefore, represents a "mild generic Calvinism" grounded in the hermeneutics of biblical inerrancy and a doctrinal stress on the divine sovereignty juxtaposed to human depravity—contra Arminian and Pelagian alternatives; salvation by Christ's penal substitution—contra exemplarist alternatives; irresistible grace—contra a soteric role for the human will; a call to mission with outcomes in personal transformation rather than systemic change; pedagogy that is didactic and word-drenched rather than experiential and visual; and a preference for expository preaching and ordered worship rather than inventive immediacies or charismatic and Pentecostal exuberances.

The dominant culture has its "purists," a few hyper-Calvinist faculty members with their student followers who are "truly Reformed" (TR), pressing toward the outer limits of sovereignty/inerrancy didacticism. But there are also acceptable variants within the normative culture that give more of a place to aggressive evangelism, the role of personal decision and affect-oriented piety.

While the foregoing culture-message is construed as dominant, a competitor is on the scene, one given impetus by the influx of students more and more shaped by parachurch movements such as Campus Crusade, InterVarsity, Navigators and Young Life, and including a vocal charismatic and Pentecostal presence. This counter-culture brings with it "praise choruses" and personal testimony, experiential preaching and evangelistic zeal. Over time, most students learn to "negotiate" with the dominant culture, not adopting it wholesale but adapting it to their past cultural commitments and future vocational settings. And there are several faculty too who are at the outer edge of Evangelical's normative culture, more so for "liberalizing" reasons than for the evangelical experientialism of incoming students. Indeed, since the research years of *Being There*, these critics-in-residence have left Evangelical.

And Mainline? Its course of study—M.Div. students and others proceeding year by year through a more common curriculum—prompts researchers Daniel Aleshire and Penny Long Marler to follow events and persons through a three-year sequence of (1) initial "encounter," (2) "working things out" and (3) "resolutions." Commentary focuses on formative faculty figures and happenings such as Dean "Harriet Hercon" and her welcome of new students, her Mission and Ministry course, and her farewell party as she leaves for scholarly work at another school (fifteen of the eighty-one pages on Mainline); the varied reactions of student and faculty to a student suicide; controversies about a sexually explicit campus art exhibit; sharp debates about inclusive language for deity; intense discussion of the victim status of ethnic communities, women, gays and lesbians, the disabled and elders; and the role of the student paper, with the special attention given to racism. Mainline's backdrop differs from Evangelical as a denominational school with older students (38 as the average age of the 1989 entering class), a larger minority group (18 percent in the 1989 class), greater diversity of theological views but half the student body affiliated with Mainline's denomination, and a faculty with much higher percentages of women and minority teachers than Evangelical.

The message heard from Mainline, a message that functions as the "map of the dominant culture's contours and boundaries," is that religious institutions should embody justice for all people and seek to transform human structures so that they are just and inclusive. . . . Inclusiveness is the means by which institutions implement justice. (208)

Racism and sexism are major concerns, with gay and lesbian and physically handicapped constituencies also "valorized." A "theology of liberation and a 'preferential option for the poor'" provide ideational warrants. Inclusive language is an important touchstone, as is diversity of representation in faculty and student body, ceremonies, committees, pictures in publication, search committees, and so on.

Like Evangelical, Mainline has its "purists," especially a number of faculties members described as "austere and rigorous" in "feminist and liberation" commitments, judging congregations and denominations "fundamentally flawed." The purist view on church institutions is to be distinguished from the school's dominant message, which holds that congregation and denomination can be changed, with the seminary geared to creating change agents.

Here too the researchers find a clash of cultures (although the description of disclosive events and persons at Mainline often appears as a commonality of student and institutional cultures). Students arrive with "many views and practices of religious communities outside the school that the school's central message opposes" (217). Over time, the justice and inclusivity message and culture have their effect to one degree or another, albeit minimally with some, who become adept at a "duck and cover" strategy. A milder "service" metaphor which students bring with them is recast in terms of "the gospel according to MTS"— "justice . . . diversity . . . inclusivity" (193). Students continue to believe that congregations and denominations will be hospitable to their efforts in doing what the seminary's normative culture says is the church's purpose: "making the world a better place to live" (218). Like their Evangelical counterparts, Mainline students develop their own "cocktails" of "creatively mixed positions" (248).

The tales told in this report of underwater life are well worth hearing. They demonstrate how much more goes on than is indicated by the ads in the seminary issues of *Christianity Today* and the *Christian Century*. *Being There* makes its case that a significant part of the preparation of the next generation of Protestant leadership happens in subsurface cultures—and their clashes—only hinted at by curriculum visibilities and institutional self-descriptions. The portraits of faculty, students and administration and the narratives of key events and disputes make for fascinating reading and serve as effective disclosure devices for what the research teams believe to be the contours and substance of each culture. For seminary administrators, faculty and trustees with plans for changing their institutions, *Being There* is a good dose of realism about where it must happen and how difficult the change efforts will prove to be.

Especially valuable is the documentation of the diversity of an evangelical world that is often assumed by outsiders to be monolithic. This includes differences within the dominant culture and the distinction between the institutional and student cultures. It is also illustrated by the Modern Theology course at Evangelical that gives firsthand encounter with major exponents of alternative views, an exposure to the "other" that has no counterpart in mainline seminaries—for all the rhetoric of inclusivity (no counterpart in the sense of a platform for major evangelical voices comparable to Evangelical's invitations to James Cone, John Cobb, David Tracy or Letty Mandeville Russell). Along with appreciation for the insights of this work, two questions persist for me: (1) Do I recognize the evangelical seminary I know? (2) Is the picture of Mainline to be taken as indicative of mainline seminaries?

On Evangelical: While Roy Parks is as influential in shaping the school's message as the researchers portray him to be, describing him as "lean . . . mean . . . austere-looking" may say more about their view of Parks's Calvinism than it does about the person. "Reg O'Neil," the partner to whom Parks is linked, and cited often as both formative and indicative of the school's normative culture, was a one-course, one-term visiting professor. He is a sociologist, not a theologian, and he has had little influence on the school. So too the chapel dean, "Andrew Watson," is assigned a representative and interpretive role in the message and culture that does not comport with his recent arrival and part-time presence at Evangelical. Several new and younger faculty get high visibility as reinforcing the sharply right-brained and Reformed image of Evangelical, but little attention is given to other long-time faculty members whose piety and theology do not fit the picture. Indeed, by portraying

Evangelical's dominant culture as essentially didactic cum scholastic, the researchers miss the accent on interiority, a conversion piety that is common to both faculty and student cultures and is one of the marks of being "evangelical." Again, while "Robert Harlan" is given the attention he is due as a "variant" presence, there is no clue that he is a remnant of the "moderate" party, most of whom departed Evangelical in the preceding years. Another puzzle: Is it true that most of the students "(like most of the faculty) pay little attention to world events unless they have religious implications" (247)? Perhaps, for the researchers, the prolife political passions of both students and faculty count only as the latter. Maybe my association over the years with both faculty and students in public issues that run from racism, urban poverty, anti-Semitism, science-technology and the perils of political fundamentalism is too limited. It is difficult, however, to imagine a culture in the Reformed tradition that is not intrinsically "world-formative" (Nicholas Wolterstorff).

On Mainline: Surely diversity/inclusivity is a mark of today's mainline seminary message. But is it the defining characteristic of its dominant culture? Whatever may be the case at Mainline, this is not true of mainline seminaries in general. My own modest research in one field, theology (I received responses and syllabi from theologians in 140 seminaries in the same time period as the research of *Being There*), shows a determined effort to retrieve the classical theological tradition as the necessary basis for justice, inclusivity and peace commitments. (See chapter four on retrieval of the tradition in mainline seminaries.) With Browning's observation in mind, it's worth remembering that "congregational studies," and derivatives such as *Being There,* were born from the womb of the very culture this work describes as "mainline." While less controlled by the characteristics attributed to it in *Being There,* a strong "liberal Protestant" strain within mainline seminaries does define the meaning of church in essentially social-ethical terms. Research so influenced would quite naturally view the role of the seminary as preparing students for "responsible citizenship" (279) and see it on a continuum of other graduate schools with the same social purpose. Such a perspective in a research typology of "liberal/conservative" would be tempted to think that the conservative culture has little concern for world affairs. In an interesting and somewhat conflicted discussion of current right/left culture-war commentary (James Davison Hunter and Robert Wuthnow), the authors agree that (1) "the two [seminaries] do divide along lines suggested by Hunter" (257) but (2) the fault-lines/culture-war "metaphors overstate the differences that we found in the two schools" (vii), and (3) other data show that there is a "large middle . . . not likely to be mobilized by either polar opposites. Our experience in the two schools support this view" (258). In spite of the latter disavowal, the bipolar schema of study and the juxtapositions expounded throughout are clearly kin to the two-party theory. As such, *Being There's* perspectival stories tend to obscure the existence of a "centrist culture" in both seminaries. This missing culture is only now getting the attention it is due, as in the important new research of Douglas Jacobsen and William Trollinger Jr. on "Re-forming the Center." (See the April 1997 issue of *Interpretation* for some of its results and a discussion of today's mainline centrist phenomenon.)

Of course, there is a difference between the cultures of mainline ("ecumenical") and evangelical seminaries and constituencies. Hermeneutically considered, it has to do with the status and role of historical context/human experience vis-à-vis the authoritative texts of the tradition. Easily identified is a "left" in which context rejects text and a "right" in which text excludes context. Often easily ignored is an increasingly vocal center-left in mainline Protestantism and a center-right in evangelicalism, both of which find a place for text and context and each treating text as magisterial and context as ministerial, albeit in degrees and ways coordinate with their evangelical and ecumenical cultures. These evangelical-ecumenical convergences have to do with the christological *Center* each accents, the doctrinal *centralities* each espouses and commitment to some kind of a *center span* of conversation across the chasm of left and right.

There is more of a center in the dominant cultures of both Evangelical and Mainline than *Being There's* two-party typology suggests, a presence discernible even in its own descriptions. The research team at Evangelical finds, indeed features, a forceful internal critique of contemporary evangelicalism, its narcissisms and intellectual vacuity. This Barthian-like assault on "culture-Protestantism" is much like comparable internal critiques of mainline religion mounted by today's self-defined centrist movements. Further, the Modern Theology course with the platform offered to major nonevangelical voices, and the entree given to other mainline persons and ideas (including a mainline theologian asked to respond to one of the invited nonevangelical voices), sits uneasily with too-simple either/or characterizations.

And at Mainline, what does this aside suggest?

A number of faculty members . . . affirm justice and inclusion but do not want it to be defined as the exclusive center of what Mainline is about. They want the center to be identified as explicitly and traditionally religious—"the historic(al) faith," according to some, or the "catholic tradition," or "the christological position." (216)

"A number of faculty members" committed to justice and inclusivity who resist the definition of their culture in solely "justice and inclusivity" terms deserve more than passing reference. This sounds much like the "both/and" message of the mainline center, a hidden history easily missed by culture-war categories. Actually (as reported to me by faculty at Mainline), the change of deans a year after the research began gave greater voice to Mainline's center and raises a caution about the prominent symbolic place assigned by the researchers to Harriet Hercon.

Worth pondering as well for the future of Protestant leadership is the acknowledgment by the authors that students in both institutions, over time, learn to "negotiate" with the perceived dominant culture, developing their own "creatively mixed positions." As such, *Being There*'s picture of evangelical/conservative/orthodoxy vs. mainline/liberal/orthopraxy needs qualification by attention to elusive constituencies that do not fit right-left partisanships. Of course, it must be said that this critique reflects my own participation in, and advocacy of, "re-forming the center."

Reinhold Niebuhr spoke of our human nature as a divine image inseparable from the "contingencies and necessities" of both nature and history. *Being There* is a salutary reminder of the role subsurface cultures play in the formation of those of us whose vocational dealings are with the *imago,* a focus that too often invites forgetfulness of our creatureliness. Yet the stewards of this sobriety are not exempt from their own contingencies and necessities. Better that both the observed and the observer acknowledge our underside lest the pretensions of the Fall compound the exigencies of our finitude.

Notes

Preface
[1]See Gabriel Fackre, "Hope's Partners: Visionaries and Futurists," *The Christian Century* 88 (September 7, 1970): 1060-63.
[2]So argued in *Ecumenical Faith in Evangelical Perspective* (Grand Rapids, Mich.: Eerdmans, 1993).

Chapter 1: Theology Ephemeral & Durable
[1]See my deployment of this schema in "Theology: Ephemeral, Conjunctural and Perennial," in *Altered Landscapes,* ed. David W. Lotz (Grand Rapids, Mich.: Eerdmans, 1989), pp. 246-67.
[2]David Halberstam, *The Fifties* (New York: Random House, 1993).
[3]Paul Tillich, *Systematic Theology* (Chicago: University of Chicago Press, 1951), 1:3-8.
[4]Will Herberg, *Protestant, Catholic, Jew* (New York: Doubleday, 1956).
[5]Gabriel Fackre and Dorothy Fackre, *Under the Steeple* (Nashville: Abingdon, 1957).
[6]Roger Shinn, *Union Seminary Tower,* Fall 1963, p. 3.
[7]For example, Jürgen Moltmann's *Theology of Hope: On the Ground and the Implications of a Christian Eschatology,* trans. James W. Leitch (London: SCM Press, 1965) and Wolfhart Pannenberg, *Jesus—God and Man,* trans. Lewis L. Wilkins and Duane Priebe (Philadelphia: Westminster Press, 1968).
[8]Harvey Cox, *The Secular City: Secularization and Urbanization in Theological Perspective,* rev. ed. (New York: Macmillan, 1965, 1966).
[9]Dietrich Bonhoeffer, *Letters and Papers from Prison,* enlarged edition, ed. Eberhard Bethge (New York: Macmillan, 1972).
[10]J. A. T. Robinson, *Honest to God* (Philadelphia: Westminster Press, 1963).
[11]Final Report of the Western European Working Group and North American Working Group of the Department on Studies in Evangelism, *The Church for Others* (Geneva: World Council of Churches, 1967).
[12]Gabriel Fackre, *Secular Impact* (Philadelphia: Pilgrim Press, 1968).
[13]Gabriel Fackre, *The Pastor and the World* (Philadelphia: Christian Education Press, 1964).
[14]Gabriel Fackre, *Humiliation and Celebration: Post-radical Themes in Doctrine, Morals and Mission* (New York: Sheed & Ward, 1969).
[15]Gabriel Fackre, *The Rainbow Sign: Christian Futurity* (London: Epworth, 1969; Grand Rapids, Mich.: Eerdmans, 1969).
[16]Harvey Cox, *The Feast of Fools: A Theological Essay on Festivity and Fantasy* (Cambridge, Mass.: Harvard University Press, 1969).
[17]Harvey Cox, *Seduction of the Spirit: The Use and Misuse of People's Religion* (New York:

Simon & Schuster, 1973).

[18]Harvey Cox, *Turning East: Why Americans Look to the Orient for Spirituality—And What That Search Can Mean to the West* (New York: Simon & Schuster, 1977).

[19]Andrew M. Greeley, *Unsecular Man: The Persistence of Religion* (New York: Schocken Books, 1972).

[20]Edward Schillebeeckx, *Jesus: An Experiment in Christology*, trans. Hubert Hoskins (New York: Seabury Press, 1979), and Edward Schillebeeckx, *Christ: The Experience of Jesus as Lord*, trans. John Bowden (New York: Seabury Press, 1980).

[21]James H. Cone, *Black Theology and Black Power* (New York: Seabury Press, 1969).

[22]James Cone, *A Black Theology of Liberation* (New York: J. B. Lippincott, 1970).

[23]Orlando E. Costas, *The Church and Its Mission: A Shattering Critique from the Third World* (Wheaton, Ill.: Tyndale, 1974).

[24]Mary Daly, *Beyond God the Father: Toward a Philosophy of Women's Liberation* (Boston: Beacon, 1973).

[25]Mary Daly, *Gyn/Ecology: The Metaethics of Radical Feminism* (Boston: Beacon, 1978).

[26]Letty M. Russell, *Human Liberation in a Feminist Perspective—A Theology* (Philadelphia: Westminster Press, 1974).

[27]Letty M. Russell, ed., *The Liberating Word: A Guide to Nonsexist Interpretation of the Bible* (Philadelphia: Westminster Press, 1976).

[28]Phyllis Trible, *God and the Rhetoric of Sexuality* (Philadelphia: Fortress, 1978).

[29]Elisabeth Schüssler Fiorenza, *In Memory of Her: A Feminist Theological Reconstruction of Christian Origins* (New York: Crossroad, 1985).

[30]Gabriel Fackre, *Do and Tell: Engagement Evangelism in the 70s* (Grand Rapids, Mich.: Eerdmans, 1973-1975).

[31]Gabriel Fackre, *Word in Deed: Theological Themes in Evangelism* (Grand Rapids, Mich.: Eerdmans, 1975).

[32]Gabriel Fackre, Dorothy Fackre and family, "A Catechism for Today's Storytellers," *Youth* 23 (July 1972): 23-42.

[33]Gabriel Fackre, *Conversations in Faith* (Philadelphia: United Church Press, 1968).

[34]Gabriel Fackre, *The Christian Story: A Narrative Interpretation of Christian Doctrine* (Grand Rapids, Mich.: Eerdmans, 1978, 2nd ed. [rev.], 1984, 3rd ed. [rev.], 1996).

[35]George A. Lindbeck, *The Nature of Doctrine: Religion and Theology in a Postliberal Age* (Philadelphia: Westminster Press, 1984).

[36]Hans Frei, *The Eclipse of the Biblical Narrative: A Study in Eighteenth- and Nineteenth-Century Hermeneutics* (New Haven, Conn.: Yale University Press, 1974).

[37]Carl F. H. Henry, *God, Revelation and Authority*, 6 vols. (Waco, Tex.: Word, 1976-1983).

[38]Gabriel Fackre, *The Christian Story: Authority—Scripture in the Church for the World* (Grand Rapids, Mich.: Eerdmans, 1987).

[39]Dorothy Fackre and Gabriel Fackre, *Christian Basics* (Grand Rapids, Mich.: Eerdmans, 1991).

[40]Gabriel Fackre, *The Religious Right and Christian Faith* (Grand Rapids, Mich.: Eerdmans, 1992-1993).

[41]S. Mark Heim, *Salvations: Truth and Difference in Religion* (Maryknoll, N.Y.: Orbis Books, 1995).

[42]A third volume appears in the Edinburgh Constructive Theology series as *The Doctrine of Revelation: A Narrative Interpretation* (Edinburgh: Edinburgh University Press, 1997; Grand Rapids, Mich.: Eerdmans, 1997).

Chapter 2: The Church of the Center

[1]H. Richard Niebuhr, *Christ and Culture* (New York: Harper & Brothers, 1951), pp. 116-20.

[2]Douglas Jacobsen and William Vance Trollinger Jr., "Evangelical and Ecumenical: Re-forming the Center," *The Christian Century* 111 (July 13-20, 1994): 682-84; Kyle A. Pasewark and Garrett E. Paul, "Forming an Emphatic Christian Center: A Call to Political Responsibility," *The Christian Century* 111 (August 24-31, 1994): 780-83; Douglas Jacobsen, "What Culture-War? The View from the Center," *The Christian Century* 112 (November 15, 1995): 1082-85; Bill J. Leonard, "When the Denominational Center Doesn't Hold: The Southern Baptist Experience," *The Christian Century* 110 (September 22-29, 1993): 905-10. See also Donald A. Luidens, "Re-centering the Church?" *Perspectives* 10 (November 1995): 17-21.

[3]The culture-war thesis is set forth in such works as Robert Wuthnow's *Restructuring of American Religion* and *The Struggle for the American Soul*, and in James Davison Hunter's *Culture Wars* and *Before the Shooting Begins*. Published papers from the early rounds of the Re-forming the Center project are forthcoming. Portions of this article were prepared for the keynote address of the final round of the project, May 31-June 1, 1996, Messiah College.

[4]Jack Rogers, *Claiming the Center* (Louisville, Ky.: Westminster John Knox Press, 1995), p. 158.

[5]Niebuhr, *Christ and Culture*, pp. 45-299.

[6]Ibid., p. 117.

[7]So confirmed by son Christopher Niebuhr in a letter to me, July 3, 1996.

[8]So argued in Gabriel Fackre, *The Promise of Reinhold Niebuhr*, 2nd ed. (Lanham, Md.: University Press of America, 1994).

[9]The difference is illustrated in a famous *Christian Century* fraternal exchange: H. Richard Niebuhr's "The Grace of Doing Nothing," and Reinhold Niebuhr's "Must We Do Nothing?" reprinted in Margaret Frakes, ed., *Christian Century Reader* (New York: Association Press, 1962), pp. 216-28, with a response by H. Richard Niebuhr, "The Only Way into the Kingdom of God," ibid., pp. 228-31.

[10]Dietrich Bonhoeffer, *Christ the Center* (New York: Harper & Row, 1966).

[11]From "The Theological Declaration of Barmen," in Arthur Cochrane, *The Church's Confession Under Hitler* (Philadelphia: Westminster Press, 1962), pp. 237-42. Hans Asmussen was assigned as codrafter, but the reports assert the substance of the Declaration to be Barth's.

[12]Rogers, *Claiming the Center*, p. 59. He understands this conviction to be grounded in the "ultimate religious worldview" of "the Christian story." Ibid., pp. 3, 159-60. For an attempt to tell this story, see Gabriel Fackre, *The Christian Story: A Narrative Interpretation of Christian Doctrine*, 3rd ed. (Grand Rapids, Mich.: Eerdmans, 1996).

[13]*Time*, October 30, 1980, p. 85.

[14]From "The Craigville Colloquy Letter to Our Brothers and Sisters in the United Church of Christ."

[15]Douglas Jacobsen and William Vance Trollinger Jr., "Re-forming What Center?" *Conference of the Re-forming the Center Project*, Messiah College, May 31-June 1, 1996.

[16]The formula advanced in *A Common Calling*, the current study document calling for "altar and pulpit fellowship" among Lutheran and Reformed constituencies in North America. See Keith F. Nickle and Timothy F. Lull, eds., *A Common Calling: The Witness of Our Reformation Churches in North America Today* (Minneapolis:

Augsburg Fortress, 1993), pp. 29-32, 66.

[17]So stressed in many of the recent works on the Trinity, as in Jürgen Moltmann, *The Trinity and the Kingdom*; Wolfhart Pannenberg, *Systematic Theology*, vol. 1; Thomas Torrance, *The Trinitarian Faith*; Colin Gunton, *The One, the Three and the Many*; Catherine Mowry LaCugna, *God for Us*; Leonardo Boff, *Trinity and Society*.

[18]George A. Lindbeck, *The Nature of Doctrine: Religion and Theology in a Postliberal Age* (Philadelphia: Westminster Press, 1984).

[19]See the recent issue of *Interpretation* on "The Resurgence of Systematic Theology," vol. 49 (July 1995).

[20]Leander Keck, *The Church Confident* (Nashville: Abingdon, 1993). Keck was the keynoter of the subsequent colloquy.

[21]Gilbert Bartholomew, Richard Floyd et al., "Confessing Christ," September 30, 1993.

[22]"An Open Letter to American Baptist Congregations and Pastors from Some Former Leaders in the ABC/USA," *In Mission* (March 1996): 13-16.

[23]See the journal *The Gospel and Our Culture*, ed. George Hunsberger, published by The Gospel and Our Culture Network.

[24]For denominational response to the *Newsweek* article, see Andy Lang, "Newsweek Denounces UCC Hymnal," UCC Home Page, World Wide Web.

[25]For a scrutiny of this spectrum, see Gabriel Fackre, "Inclusivity: The Language Debate," *Prism: A Theological Forum of the United Church of Christ* 9 (Spring 1994): 52-65.

[26]Richard Christensen, ed., *How Shall We Sing the Lord's Song?* (Pittsburgh: Pickwick Press, 1997).

[27]Tony Campolo, *Can Mainline Churches Make a Comeback?* (Valley Forge, Penn.: Judson Press, 1995). See also Rogers, *Claiming the Center*, pp. 158-75.

[28]See Consultation on Church Union, *Churches in Covenant Communion*, rev. ed. (Princeton, N.J.: Consultation on Church Union, 1995).

[29]A case in point, again, is the UCC. The two most active Conference Ministers in Confessing Christ have been notable among their peers for advancing the Lutheran-Reformed Conversation and COCU.

[30]Note, for example, the Ecunet meetings *Confessing Christ* and *The Covenant of Agreement*.

[31]Timothy R. Phillips and Dennis L. Okholm, eds., *The Nature of Confession: Evangelicals and Postliberals in Conversation* (Downers Grove, Ill.: InterVarsity Press, 1996).

[32]I argue for this convergence in *Ecumenical Faith in Evangelical Perspective* (Grand Rapids, Mich.: Eerdmans, 1993).

Chapter 3: Centralities in the Parish

[1]On the history of Christian education as traced back to the patristic period, see Kendig Brubaker Cully, ed., *Basic Writings in Christian Education* (Philadelphia: Westminster Press, 1960).

[2]This widespread movement called "Confessing Christ," now establishing centers of theological study in churches around the country, appeared as such a departure from standard perceptions and practices of mainline Protestantism that stories immediately appeared on the wire services (AP and RNS). Information on it is available from Dr. Frederick Trost, Conference Minister, Wisconsin Conference, UCC, DeForest, Wisconsin.

[3]Leander Keck, *The Church Confident: Christianity Can Repent but It Must Not Whimper*

(Nashville: Abingdon, 1993).

[4]Milton J. Coalter, John M. Mulder and Louis B. Weeks, eds., *The Presbyterian Presence: The Twentieth-Century Experience*, 7 vols. (Philadelphia: Westminster/John Knox Press).

[5]David Wells, *No Place for Truth: Or, Whatever Happened to Evangelical Theology?* (Grand Rapids, Mich.: Eerdmans, 1993).

[6]See the survey of the teaching of systematics in 150 seminaries and divinity schools, Gabriel Fackre, "The State of Systematics," *Dialog* 31 (Winter 1992): 54-61.

[7]For a review of the offerings and a history of the trend see Gabriel Fackre, "In Quest of the Comprehensive: The Systematics Revival," *Religious Studies Review* 20 (January 1994): 7-12; and Gabriel Fackre, "The Surge in Systematics," *The Journal of Religion* 73 (April 1993): 223-37.

[8]The theological commonplaces are the structure of a small work for congregational study written several years ago: Dorothy and Gabriel Fackre, *Christian Basics: A Primer for Pilgrims* (Grand Rapids, Mich.: Eerdmans, 1998, 5th printing), with accompanying videotapes and workbook, Andover Newton Theological School.

[9]As in Bernhard W. Anderson's durable educational resource, *The Unfolding Drama of the Bible*, 3rd ed. (Philadelphia: Fortress Press, 1988).

[10]See the discussion of this development in Stanley J. Grenz and Roger E. Olson, *20th-Century Theology: God and the World in a Transitional Age* (Downers Grove, Ill.: InterVarsity Press, 1992), pp. 271-85.

[11]For perspective on the latter coordinate with these comments, see Gabriel Fackre, *The Christian Story*, vol. 2, *Authority: Scripture in the Church for the World* (Grand Rapids, Mich.: Eerdmans, 1987).

[12]For important developments in Latin American liberation and feminist theologies, as well as the earlier theologies of hope, that are seeking to draw out the social-justice implications of the classical teaching, see Leonardo Boff, *Trinity and Society*, trans. Paul Burns (Maryknoll, N.Y.: Orbis, 1988); Catherine Mowry LaCugna, *God for Us: The Trinity and Christian Life* (San Francisco: Harper, 1991); and the pioneering work by Jürgen Moltmann, *The Trinity and the Kingdom: The Doctrine of God*, trans. Margaret Kohl (San Francisco: Harper and Row, 1981).

[13]For a profound scrutiny of biblical teaching on angels, see Karl Barth, *Church Dogmatics*, III/3, trans. G. W. Bromiley and T. F. Torrance (Edinburgh: T & T Clark, 1960), pp. 369-531.

[14]Karl Menninger, *Whatever Became of Sin?* (New York: Hawthorne Books, 1973).

[15]For a survey of current church thinking see World Council of Churches, *The Theology of the Churches and the Jewish People: Statements by the World Council of Churches and its Member Churches* (Geneva: WCC Publications, 1988).

Chapter 5: I Believe in the Resurrection of the Body

[1]Reinhold Niebuhr, *Beyond Tragedy* (New York: Scribners, 1937), pp. 289-90. Niebuhr develops this theme further in his Gifford Lectures, *The Nature and Destiny of Man*, vol. 2, *Human Destiny* (New York: Scribner's, 1945), pp. 294-98. While A. Michael Ramsey cites Niebuhr's testimony approvingly in his important work *The Resurrection of Christ* (Philadelphia: Westminster Press, 1946), p. 103, critics have argued that he was less clear about where he stood on the physical resurrection of Christ.

[2]For a review of the philosophical and scientific reconsiderations see William C. Placher, *Unapologetic Theology* (Louisville, Ky.: Westminster John Knox Press),

passim. Alisdair MacIntyre in *Whose Justice? Which Rationality?* (Notre Dame, Ind.:
University of Notre Dame Press, 1988) gives a detailed analysis of how purportedly
universal judgments of reason show the marks of their social history.

[3]Bruce Marshall makes a good case that the thought of George Lindbeck, who gave
currency to a cultural-linguistic understanding of doctrine in *The Nature of Doctrine,*
does not deny propositional truth claims. See his "Aquinas as a Post-liberal Theologian," *The Thomist* 53 (July 1989): 353-402, and Lindbeck's agreeable "Response to
Bruce Marshall," pp. 403-6.

[4]As for example, the 800,000 copies of John Walvoord's *Armageddon, Oil and the Middle
East Crisis* (Grand Rapids, Mich.: Zondervan, 1991) sold during the 1991 Gulf War.

[5]Herman Kahn and Anthony J. Wiener, *The Year 2000: A Framework for Speculating
on the Next Thirty-three Years* (New York: Macmillan, 1967), passim.

[6]While John Hick's syncretistic views bear little resemblance to the position set forth
here, he effectively exposes the weakness of this latter secular eschatology, drawing
on the thought of Hans Morgenthau: John Hick, *Death and Eternal Life* (New York:
Harper & Row, 1976), pp. 87-90.

[7]The "I . . . not I" explored with profundity by Donald Baillie in *God Was in Christ*
(New York: Scribner's, 1948), pp. 106-32.

[8]See the discussion of same in Clark Pinnock and Delwin Brown, *Theological Crossfire:
An Evangelical-Liberal Dialogue* (Grand Rapids, Mich.: Zondervan, 1990), pp. 225-31. An
interesting report on "the dark side" of eschatology in American culture and theology,
including a discussion of annhilationism among evangelicals, is found in Jeffrey L.
Sheler, "Hell's Sober Comeback," *U.S. News & World Report,* March 25, 1991, pp. 56-90.

[9]Note especially Moltmann's "systematic contributions" in the series he has identified
as "Messianic Theology" (*Trinity and the Kingdom, God in Creation, The Way of Jesus
Christ, The Spirit of Life* and *The Coming of God*).

[10]For a review of these refrains in the history of Christian thought, see Brian
Hebblethwaite, *The Christian Hope* (Grand Rapids, Mich.: Eerdmans, 1984).

[11]I have explored the Advent texts in this fashion in "Vision of Shalom and Hope of
Glory," in *Social Themes of the Christian Year,* ed. Dieter Hessel (Philadelphia: Geneva
Press, 1983), pp. 32-39.

[12]Best known is Hal Lindsey, *The Late Great Planet Earth.* For a look at the disputes
within the premillennial camp see Dave MacPherson's *The Great Rapture Hoax*
(Fletcher, N.C.: New Puritan Library, 1983), which traces the origins of John Nelson
Darby's thought on this subject to the 1830 "revelations" of one Margaret Macdonald
of Scotland.

[13]On this see Karl Barth, *Church Dogmatics,* IV/3, first half, trans. and ed. G. W.
Bromiley and T. F. Torrance (Edinburgh: T & T Clark, 1961), pp. 477-78.

[14]On Protestant orthodoxy and the soul, see Heinrich Heppe, *Reformed Dogmatics,* rev.
ed., ed. Ernst Bizer, trans. G. T. Thomson with a foreword by Karl Barth (Grand
Rapids, Mich.: Baker Book House, 1978), pp. 695-701.

[15]As in the famous work by Oscar Cullmann, *Immortality of the Soul or Resurrection of
the Dead?* (New York: Macmillan, 1958). But the notion persists in Roman Catholic
theology and elsewhere. See Edmund Fortman, *Everlasting Life After Death* (New
York: Alba House, 1976), pp. 42-156.

[16]I have tried to make a case for four exegetical moves as the quest for the common,
critical, canonical and contextual senses of a text in *The Christian Story,* vol. 2,
Authority: Scripture in the Church for the World (Grand Rapids, Mich.: Eerdmans,

1987), pp. 157-390.

Chapter 6: Angels Heard & Demons Seen

[1]So the major stories on angels in the December 27, 1993, issues of both *Time* and *Newsweek*, the May 1994 two-hour network special on the same, etc.

[2]On current angel experiences, see Sophy Burnham, *A Book of Angels: Reflections on Angels Past and Present and True Stories of How They Touch Our Lives* (New York: Ballantine Books, 1990).

[3]Karl Barth, *Church Dogmatics*, III/3, ed. G. W. Bromiley and T. F. Torrance, trans. G. W. Bromiley and R. J. Ehrlich (Edinburgh: T & T Clark, 1960), p. 514.

[4]Ibid., pp. 369-531.

[5]Ibid., p. 424.

[6]Ibid., pp. 433, 437.

[7]On the interpretation of the Genesis verse and its linkage with the ancient creeds, especially the Nicene: "We believe in one God, the Father, the Almighty, maker of heaven and earth, of all that is seen and unseen," see Mortimer J. Adler, *The Angels and Us* (New York: Macmillan, 1982), pp. 37-40.

[8]Barth questions St. Thomas's philosophical reading of the "heavenlies," and Thomist interpreter Mortimer Adler in his widely read book *The Angels and Us* declares Barth, in turn, to be too restricted to Scripture and thus apologetically weak (pp. 26-29). While Barth has a better biblical compass and can steer us between the Scylla of New Age angelologies and the Charybdis of Enlightenment orthodoxies, there are significant convergences between the views of both. Also, here and there Adler appears to be more faithful to the biblical accounts, as in the symmetry of creation's nature, human nature and supernature.

[9]Both Christian art and traditional theology have contributed much to these preoccupations. For a review of them see Theodore Ward, *Men and Angels* (New York: Viking, 1969), passim.

[10]Ibid., p. 451.

[11]Barth, *Church Dogmatics*, III/3, pp. 519-31.

[12]Ibid., pp. 492-93.

[13]For an illuminating trail of teaching from the Fathers on the mission of angels—the law, world religions, nativity, ascension, church, sacraments, death, etc.—see Jean Daniélou, *The Angels and Their Mission: According to the Fathers of the Church*, trans. David Heimann (Westminster, Md.: Christian Classics, 1976).

[14]Barth, indeed, somewhat grudgingly acknowledges some truth in Peterson's doxological stress. See *Church Dogmatics*, III/3, p. 483.

[15]*Heidelberg Catechism* (Grand Rapids, Mich.: CRC Publications, 1988), Question 31.

[16]On the prophetic office as part of the doctrine of the Atonement, see Gabriel Fackre, "Atonement," in *Encyclopedia of the Reformed Faith*, ed. Donald McKim (Louisville, Ky.: Westminster John Knox Press, 1992); and Fackre, *The Christian Story*, rev. ed. (Grand Rapids, Mich.: Eerdmans, 1984), pp. 135-54.

[17]Barth, *Church Dogmatics*, III/3, p. 373.

[18]Ibid., p. 477.

[19]*Heidelberg Catechism*, Question 32.

[20]Leander E. Keck, *The Church Confident: Christianity Can Repent but It Must Not Whimper* (Nashville: Abingdon, 1993), p. 34.

[21]Ibid., pp. 36-37.

[22]David Wells, *No Place for Truth: Or, Whatever Happened to Evangelical Theology?* (Grand Rapids, Mich.: Eerdmans, 1993).

[23]The eucharistic prayer and seraphic hymn, Order for Holy Communion, *The Hymnal,* Evangelical and Reformed Church (St. Louis, Mo.: Eden Publishing House, 1947), p. 25.

[24]*Heidelberg Catechism,* Question 31.

[25]The subtitle of her *A Book of Angels.*

[26]John Calvin, *Institutes of the Christian Religion,* ed. John T. McNeill, trans. Ford Lewis Battles (Philadelphia: Westminster Press, 1960), 1:167.

[27]Ibid., p. 170.

[28]Francis Thompson, "The Kingdom of God."

[29]Walter Wink, *Naming the Powers* (Philadelphia: Fortress, 1984), *Unmasking the Powers* (Philadelphia: Fortress, 1986) and *Engaging the Powers* (Minneapolis: Fortress, 1992).

[30]Wink, *Naming the Powers,* pp. 104-5.

[31]See Gabriel Fackre, "Elements of a Theology of Institutions" (Center for the Ministry of the Laity, Andover Newton Theological School, 1985, mimeographed). Richard Broholm, founder of this center and pioneer in the interpretation of the workplace ministry of the laity, is making fruitful use of Wink's categories in developing a theology of institutions.

[32]Robert Webber in *The Church in the World* (Grand Rapids, Mich.: Zondervan, 1986) strives to hold together the structural and the ontological dimensions of powers and principalities.

[33]See Albert H. Van den Heuvel, *These Rebellious Powers* (New York: Friendship Press, 1965). Pioneering work was done by George Caird, *Principalities and Powers* (Oxford: Clarendon Press, 1956), and Hendrikus Berkhof, *Christ and the Powers,* trans. John Howard Yoder (Scottdale, Penn.: Herald, 1962).

[34]Paul Tillich, *The Religious Situation,* trans. H. Richard Niebuhr (New York: Henry H. Holt, 1932).

[35]Reinhold Niebuhr, *Moral Man and Immoral Society* (New York: Scribner's, 1932).

[36]C. S. Lewis, *The Screwtape Letters* (New York: Macmillan, 1944).

[37]Karl Barth, *A Letter to Great Britain from Switzerland* (London: Sheldon Press, 1941), pp. 10-11.

[38]Clinton Arnold's careful study *Powers of Darkness: Principalities and Powers in Paul's Letters* (Downers Grove, Ill.: InterVarsity Press, 1992) makes a strong evangelical case for the personal ontology of the "dark powers" but forcefully asserts the "defeat of the powers at the cross" (pp. 100-109) and challenges apocalyptic preoccupations with the devil's present rule. In a similar vein see also J. I. Packer, "The Devil's Dossier," *Christianity Today* 37 (June 21, 1993): 24.

[39]John Milton, "Hymn on the Morning of Christ's Nativity."

Chapter 9: Whither Evangelicalism?

[1]With papers published in Timothy Phillips and Dennis Okholm, eds., *The Nature of Confession* (Downers Grove, Ill.: InterVarsity Press, 1996).

[2]See Gabriel Fackre, "Evangelical, Evangelicalism," in *The Westminster Dictionary of Christian Theology,* rev. ed., ed. Alan Richardson and John Bowden (Philadelphia: Westminster Press, 1983), pp. 191-92.

[3]See "Ways of Inclusivity," *Prism: A Theological Forum of the United Church of Christ* 9 (Spring 1994): 52-65.

Chapter 11: IBM & the Incognito Christ
[1]See the comments on Wink in chapter six.

Chapter 13: The Continuing Relevance of Reinhold Niebuhr
[1]Alan Paton, "Journey Continued: An Autobiography," reprinted in *Kent Quarterly* 9 (Fall 1989): 30, quoted in Ronald H. Stone, *Professor Reinhold Niebuhr: A Mentor to the Twentieth Century* (Louisville, Ky.: Westminster John Knox Press, 1992), p. 133.
[2]Mark Ellingsen, "Niebuhr for the 90s? Towards a Lutheran Revival," *Lutheran Forum* 27 (May 1993): 40-43.
[3]Dennis P. McCann, "The Case for Christian Realism: Rethinking Reinhold Niebuhr," *The Christian Century* 112 (June 7-14, 1995): 604-7.
[4]Charles C. Brown, *Niebuhr and His Age: Reinhold Niebuhr's Prophetic Role in the Twentieth Century* (Philadelphia: Trinity Press International, 1992), and *A Reinhold Niebuhr Reader: Selected Essays, Articles and Reviews,* comp. and ed. Charles C. Brown (Philadelphia: Trinity Press International, 1992).
[5]Arthur Schlesinger Jr., in *The New York Times,* June 22, 1992, p. A17.
[6]For my description and assessment of this phenomenon, see *The Religious Right and Christian Faith* (Grand Rapids, Mich.: Eerdmans, 1982); and "Political Fundamentalism," in *Theology, Politics and Peace,* ed. Theodore Runyon (Maryknoll, N.Y.: Orbis Books, 1989), pp. 117-25.
[7]On these matters, see Gabriel Fackre, *The Doctrine of Revelation: A Narrative Interpretation* (Grand Rapids, Mich.: Eerdmans, 1997), pp. 120-52.
[8]Reinhold Niebuhr, *The Nature and Destiny of Man: A Christian Interpretation,* 2 vols. (New York: Scribner's, 1941-1943), 2:211.
[9]Reinhold Niebuhr, *Beyond Tragedy* (New York: Scribner's, 1937), pp. 189-90. See also *Nature and Destiny of Man,* 2:294-98.